Open Access Musicology

VOLUME ONE

Edited by

Daniel Barolsky and Louis Epstein

**LEVER
PRESS**

The complete manuscript of this work was subjected to a fully closed ("double blind") review process. For more information, please see our Peer Review Commitments and Guidelines at https://www.leverpress.org/peerreview

DOI: https://doi.org/10.3998/mpub.12063224
Print ISBN: 978-1-64315-021-5
Open access ISBN: 978-1-64315-022-2

Published in the United States of America by Lever Press, in partnership with Amherst College Press and Michigan Publishing

Contents

Member Institution Acknowledgments

Lever Press is a joint venture. This work was made possible by the generous support of Lever Press member libraries from the following institutions:

Adrian College
Agnes Scott College
Allegheny College
Amherst College
Bard College
Berea College
Bowdoin College
Carleton College
Claremont Graduate
    University
Claremont McKenna College
Clark Atlanta University
Coe College
College of Saint Benedict /
    Saint John's University
The College of Wooster

Denison University
DePauw University
Earlham College
Furman University
Grinnell College
Hamilton College
Harvey Mudd College
Haverford College
Hollins University
Keck Graduate Institute
Kenyon College
Knox College
Lafayette College Library
Lake Forest College
Macalester College
Middlebury College

Morehouse College
Oberlin College
Pitzer College
Pomona College
Rollins College
Santa Clara University
Scripps College
Sewanee: The University of the
    South
Skidmore College
Smith College
Spelman College
St. Lawrence University

St. Olaf College
Susquehanna University
Swarthmore College
Trinity University
Union College
University of Puget Sound
Ursinus College
Vassar College
Washington and Lee
    University
Whitman College
Willamette University
Williams College

Preface

In the fall of 2015, a collection of faculty at liberal arts colleges began a conversation about the challenges we faced as instructors: Why were there so few course materials accessible to undergraduates and lay readers that reflected current scholarly debate? How can we convey the relevance of studying music history to current and future generations of students? And how might we represent and reflect the myriad, often conflicting perspectives, positions, and identities that make up both music's history and the writers of history?

Here we offer one response to those questions. *Open Access Musicology* is a free collection of essays, written in an accessible style and with a focus on modes of inquiry rather than content coverage. Our authors draw from their experience as scholars but also as teachers. They have been asked to describe why they became musicologists in the first place and how their individual paths led to the topics they explore and the questions they pose. Like most scholarly literature, the essays have all been reviewed by experts in the field. Unlike all scholarly literature, the essays have also been reviewed by students at a variety of institutions for clarity and relevance.

These essays are intended for undergraduates, graduate students, and interested readers without any particular expertise. They can be incorporated into courses on a range of topics as standalone readings or used to supplement textbooks. The topics introduce and explore a variety of subjects, practices, and methods but, above all, seek to stimulate classroom discussion on music history's relevance to performers, listeners, and citizens. *Open Access Musicology* will never pretend to present complete histories, cover all elements of a subject, or satisfy the agenda of every reader. Rather, each essay provides an opening to further contemplation and study. We invite readers to follow the thematic links between essays, pursue notes or other online resources provided by authors, or simply repurpose the essay's questions into new and exciting forms of research and creativity.

– Daniel Barolsky (Editor) and Louis Epstein (Associate Editor)

Acknowledgments

A new undertaking always requires a leap of faith, but this undertaking—making cutting-edge scholarship accessible and freely available for use in undergraduate classrooms—was unprecedented enough that it required a greater leap than usual. The editors are grateful to so many individuals and institutions who made that leap with us. Early work on this project was supported by a Faculty Career Enhancement Program grant from the Associated Colleges of the Midwest (ACM) in collaboration with the Andrew W. Mellon Foundation, and later by the ACM in collaboration with the Teagle Foundation. Many thanks to Brian Williams and Ed Finn at the ACM for their help along the way. In addition, St. Olaf College and Beloit College provided various kinds of support, logistical as well as financial, and our colleagues' enthusiasm for the project has sustained us at various times.

We were lucky to find kindred spirits in the burgeoning open-access publishing world. At Lever Press and the University of Michigan Press, Mark Edington, Mary Francis, and Rebecca Welzenbach provided critical support in the early stages of the project, and Beth Bouloukos and Amanda Karby shepherded us through the publication process. We are also grateful to Eden Kaiser and David Wilson for their eagle-eyed copyediting.

The Editorial Board of *Open Access Musicology*—Ryan Raul Bañagale (Colorado College), Sara Ceballos (Lawrence University), Sarah Day-O'Connell (Skidmore College), Sara Haefeli (Ithaca College), Eric Hung (Rider University and Music of Asian America Research Center), Mary Natvig (Bowling Green State University), and Anna Schultz (University of Chicago)—deserves special recognition for behind-the-scenes work, including peer reviews, author recruitment, and various kinds of institutional support, often financial. We thank our Advisory Board, too, for their advice and support.

We are grateful to those who posed insightful questions and offered feedback at presentations on *Open Access Musicology* at the 2017 Teaching Music History Conference in Boston and at the 2017 meeting of the American Musicological Society in Rochester.

Open Access Musicology was partly inspired by presentations by Sara Haefeli and Mary Natvig at the 2015 Teaching Music History Conference. After the conference, Daniel Barolsky first developed the idea through conversations with Sara, Louis Epstein, and others, but it never would have gotten underway without the crucial, early interventions of Ryan Bañagale and Sara Ceballos, who joined Daniel and Louis at the University of Chicago in August 2016 to jumpstart the project.

Finally, we express our profound gratitude to all those who reviewed the essays in this inaugural collection, including not just our scholarly peer reviewers but also dozens of teachers and students: you made this work better. And to the authors whose fabulous work we are proud to present here, we thank you for your hard work, your patience, and your willingness to take that leap of faith with us. You are making musicology better.

Daniel Barolsky, Editor
Louis Epstein, Associate Editor
November 2020

CRACKING THE CODE

What Notation Can Tell Us About Our Musical Values

S. Andrew Granade

As an undergraduate student, I knew the word musicology *as my high school piano teacher was a musicologist, but I didn't know much beyond the word. With two historians as parents (my mother taught high school and my father college), I was already oriented toward a love of history, but thought I wanted to be a pianist. That career path changed when my collegiate piano teacher began asking me questions about the background of composers I was learning and their styles. I came to love digging in the library and ultimately chose musicology for my graduate studies.*

I also developed a fascination with music of the present and recent past—as a pianist, I felt it spoke to my current life in a deeper way than music from earlier centuries, and I enjoyed the challenge of figuring out how to play effectively with a tape recording or deciphering a cryptic graphic notation. Then I discovered that a series of nondescript metal filing cabinets in the music library of my graduate school held the letters, manuscripts, and even personal effects of the

US composer Harry Partch.[1] Holding those documents in my hand for a class project electrified me, and I discovered I had many questions: How did he create his musical system? How did you play his instruments and what did his notation look like? And, most importantly, why did he throw out centuries of musical traditions to invent his own? That last question—looking into what the cultural, societal, and personal conditions are that drive a person to create the way they do—has continued to animate my work since that time, whether I'm writing about Harry Partch, music in science-fiction Westerns, or even music history pedagogy.[2] Hopefully it animates the discussion of notation that follows.

When I was a kid, sitting in my neighbor's front living room swinging my legs from the piano bench and slowly moving through finger exercises in my *Bastien Piano Basics, Level One* piano book, I never gave much thought to the black dots that filled the pages of that lavender-covered book. I was more concerned with whether my five-finger position should start on C or on G than what those notes might be communicating. But as I moved into high school and then collegiate piano study, I began to wonder how notation worked because my teachers stressed following every marking a composer made so I could accurately recreate that composer's vision and intention. They called this practice "fidelity to the score," always intoned with solemnity and reverence. Therefore, you can imagine my confusion when, as a first-year student working on Frédéric Chopin's Prelude in C minor, Op. 28, No. 20," I discovered that different editions had different markings. You can see two of these editions (one edited by Theodor Kullak and the other by Ignacy Jan Paderewski) in figures 1a and 1b. Can you spot the differences? The first example has a tempo marking (♩ = 66) missing from the second example, a crescendo that ends two beats earlier and uses treble instead of bass clef in the upper stave.[3] Then look in the third measure where the final chord has an E-flat in one edition and an E natural in the other. I remember asking my teacher which one was Chopin's version and which was the fake. Where do I stop the crescendo? Was that final chord C major or C minor? I assumed that, like in Plato's allegory of the cave, there was one pure form of a piece of music that came directly from the composer.[4] Therefore, if I wanted to be true to the composer's intent, it seemed obvious I should use that one pure version. My teacher patiently responded that Chopin often sent different versions of the same piece to different publishers, resulting in an abundance of options but no one correct version.

Figure 1a. Chopin, "Prelude in C Minor, Op. 28, No. 20," Theodor Kullak, ed., *Klavierwerke*, vol. 2: *Preludes* (Berlin: Schlesinger'sche Buch- und Musikhandlung, 1882).

Figure 1b. Chopin, "Prelude in C Minor, Op. 28, No. 20," Ignacy Jan Paderewski, Ludwik Bronarski, and Józef Turczyński, eds., *Dzieła wszystkie Fryderyka Chopina*, vol. 1: *Preludes* (Warszawa: Polskie Wydawnictwo Muzyczne, 1949).

I was floored by this revelation. My teacher must have noticed my stunned expression because we began discussing how notation works and how composers communicate through their notation.

He began assigning me works that used unusual notation just to stretch me as a musician. At my next lesson, he told me to go to the library and check out George Crumb's *Makrokosmos*, volume 2 (if this collection of piano works is unfamiliar, there is a wonderful video of Fabio Alvarez performing the collection where you can see the score as he plays).[5] In the collection, Crumb notated every fourth piece graphically to represent the work's title. For example, he wrote the cycle's final piece, "Agnus Dei," in the shape of a peace sign since the final line of the "Agnus Dei" in the Roman Catholic mass is "Lamb of God, who takes away the sins of the world, grant us peace" (see figure 2).

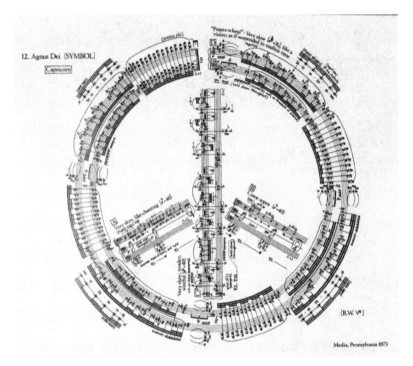

Figure 2. "Angus Dei" from Makrokosmos, Volume II by George Crumb © Copyright 1973 by C.F. Peters Corporation. All Rights Reserved.

After Crumb, I quickly branched out, and for my junior recital I performed John Corigliano's *Fantasia on an Ostinato*.[6] In the work's middle section, Corigliano wrote a series of patterns bracketed by repeat signs with the direction: "The number of repetitions is left to the imagination and sense of proportion of the performer. . . . Nothing should last too long."[7] Forget multiple Chopin versions of one piece, here was a composer opening up his work to the creative choices of the performer, leaving aspects of the piece indeterminate. By this time, I was hooked, and Corigliano's aleatoric or chance-oriented practices of leaving aspects for the performer to determine led me to John Cage, Morton Feldman, and other composers collected under the avant-garde banner who began this notation revolution in the twentieth century. Paging through John Cage's *Notations*, which featured scores he collected from friends and colleagues to show the state of notation in 1969 (all of *Notations*[8] is available for download), I discovered questions that convinced me to study musicology when I went to graduate school and have shaped my research into composers who experiment with musical practices to the present day.

I'd like to share two of the questions about notation that excite me as a musician and musicologist and then, for the rest of this essay, explore some possible answers to those questions and see what those answers tell us about what Western Europe and the Americas value in music. These questions are often glossed over (if they are even discussed) in most music curricula in the United States, as we often think about notation the way I thought about Chopin's music; namely, as a fixed entity that is universally known and used. However, many composers in the tradition of so-called Western classical music struggle against its notational system, which leads to my first question: *How does notation guide musical change?* Often, alterations and additions to this notational system arose because composers were frustrated with its limits. In his remarkable book *Sketch of a New Esthetic in Music*, the composer Ferruccio Busoni addressed this problem head-on, writing, "To the lawgivers, the signs themselves are the most important matter, and they are continually growing in their estimation; the new art of music is derived from the old signs—and these now stand for the musical art itself."[9] If we want a new music, Busoni implies, we must leave behind the old signs, or the old notation. Similarly, Harry Partch, an American composer who wanted to expand the scale beyond twelve chromatic pitches in equal temperament (e.g., the twelve pitches within any octave on a piano) to forty-three pitches in just intonation, encountered this frustration again and again as he tried to notate his justly tuned music. He remarked in his treatise *Genesis of a Music* that

> our system of notation must be held partially responsible for the inelasticity of our present musical theory, and for the misdirection of many intonational ideas that have been proposed—it is so 'easy' for the notation of 'quartertones,' for example.[10] But historically, in the establishment of current musical habits, there was little if any causal relation. Significant developments in notation, naturally enough, followed the development of musical artifices.[11]

Partch presents the inverse of Busoni: notation only changes after musical practices change.

My first question focused on composers and how they put music down on paper. My second question turns its attention to the interpretation of those notes: *How does notation impact the way performers play a piece of music?* The composer Morton Feldman, who began his career trying out new notations to elicit new sounds, remarked, "The degree to which a music's notation is responsible for much of the composition itself is one of history's best-kept secrets."[12] Notation has a psychological impact on the ways in which we approach music, a fact borne out in John Sloboda's fascinating book *Exploring the Musical Mind*. Sloboda, a British psychologist, has studied how our minds process musical notation for forty years. He points out that when musicians "read" a score, they are not simply translating sight to sound; instead, they often translate sight to meaning, subconsciously making choices

based on visual cues so the notes make musical sense based on past experience.[13] Change those visual cues and you can fundamentally change the meaning the performer attempts to communicate.

The rest of this essay explores these two questions in two ways. First, we'll skim through the history of Western European and American notational systems to see if we can discover if changes in notation come before or after musical change. Then, I want to focus on notational experiments in the twentieth century to see how and why composers stretched and modified notation and how performers have responded to those changes. By the end, we can understand more fully how different types of notation work and confirm Feldman's observation that it is an overlooked aspect of musical style.

HOW DID WE GET HERE AGAIN?

As we begin our chronology of notation, I want to present a quick caveat that I am focusing my discussion on Western musical notation because it is the type of notation in which I have training and to which the composers I study reacted. Our world has many rich and varied notational systems, any of which could be the focus of a compelling study, and if this subject seems fascinating, consider the millennia of notational practices in India or China or even tablature in Western Europe and the Americas for projects while in school.

Now to our first question: How has notation guided musical change? To answer that question, we need to have some idea of why musicians began writing down music in the first place. After all, there are plenty of musicians who cannot read notation and yet make beautiful music. Although both Greek and Roman civilizations wrote down some of their music, the early developments of many modern notational systems are found in the Christian church. One of the earliest examples of notation that survives comes from the Monastery of St. Gall in the eastern portion of what is today Switzerland. In the eleventh century, a monk named "Hartker" copied out an antiphonary[14] that not only contained the words to the antiphons the monks sang during the Divine Office, but also dots and lines and squiggles above the words that show us the melodic shape the monks sang along with those words (see figure 3). Why did Hartker do this? In the prologue to the so-called Antiphonary of Hartker of St. Gall (St. Allen Stiftbibliothek 390–91) the author wrote that singers should "devote careful attention to the right sounds."[15] In other words, monks began writing music down out of reverence for God. A monk's job was to bring his best to God, and to do so he needed to have the right notes written down and sing them in the right way.

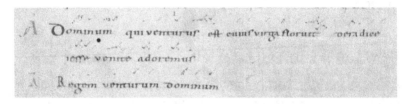

Figure 3. Gustav Scherrer, "Antiphonarium officii (Antiphonary for liturgy of the hours)," (Switzerland: Stiftsbibliothek, 1875), https://www.e-codices.unifr.ch/en/list/one/csg/0390.

These shapes are called "neumes" and evidently served as mnemonics for singers more than a way to teach new melodies. Monks did not learn how to sing the antiphons from these books but were reminded how to sing melodies they already knew by seeing the neumes. From our modern perspective, we might think that this kind of notation is narrow in use. After all, it doesn't tell us the exact pitch a singer should use nor the relationship between pitches that follow each other. However, these small dots and lines inserted into the space above the words offer a glimpse into a huge tradition surrounding musical performance in the medieval period. We have difficulty understanding how the monks' entire musical ecosystem worked because they did not spend their time writing treatises on musical performance, but in Hartker's writing we can delineate aspects of the Catholic musical system that still resonate in our own musical world.[16] What are those aspects? As Thomas Forrest Kelly noted, "First, that this is music meant to go with words; and second, that the basic unit of music-writing is not the note but the syllable."[17]

Let's zero in on that first aspect, that music was connected to words and not instrumentally derived. Consider the difference between an instrumental melody as opposed to a vocal one. Vocal melodies are, for lack of a better word, singable: they usually move in more stepwise motion, have smaller ranges, and are more regular in their rhythm than instrumental melodies. Medieval chants were intended to be sung and were more concerned with subtleties in pitch and harmony than in rhythm and meter, and that is the focus of notation in the century following the Antiphonary of Hartker. Even so, writers began to despair over substandard singing in spite of the neumes and wished for a way to precisely notate the pitches monks were to sing. Among those writers, perhaps no one wished more fervently for a clear-cut notation than Guido of Arezzo, who wrote in the *Prologus* to his own antiphonary, "In our times, of all men, singers are the most foolish."[18]

Guido was a Benedictine monk who lived and worked at the beginning of the second millennium. Early in his career, he became famous for teaching chants to young monks in record time through a new system of notation. What was the basis of that system? Horizontal lines:

The notes are so arranged, then, that each sound, however often it may be repeated in a melody, is found always in its own row. And in order that you may better distinguish these rows, lines are drawn close together, and some rows of sounds occur on the lines themselves, others in the intervening intervals or spaces. All the sounds on one line or in one space sound alike.[19]

Essentially, Guido's innovations were to have the lines drawn close together, use colors to distinguish those lines, and add clef signs to help singers locate pitches. Recent scholarship has shown that Guido did not come up with these innovations on his own but synthesized practices already in use into a clear pedagogical and notational system that survives today as the musical staff.[20]

Spreading staff notation far and wide was enough to make Guido one of the most famous monks of the medieval period. But he did not stop there. His second innovation is the one that made his *Micrologus* one of the most widely known and copied music treatises of the age and allowed singing by sight. Guido noticed that the hymn "Ut queant laxis" had a unique feature: each musical phrase begins on a pitch one step higher than the one preceding it. He decided that it made sense to label those six notes by the syllable connected to it in the hymn. Since the hymn's text to those phrases is

Ut queant laxis
Resonare fibris
Mira gestorum
Famuli tuorum
Solve pollutes
Labii reatum

Guido named the pitches "Ut, Re, Mi, Fa, Sol, La," the origins of our solfège syllables that, besides the change of "Ut" to Do" for ease of singing, remain with us.[21] Think of the simplicity of this system and how it allows a singer to see quickly what pitch they should be singing. It was a revolution and a short hop from there to other writers applying letters (ABCDEFG) in a repeating pattern to the scale's pitches.[22]

There are problems with Guido's innovations. When we stop to think about it, assigning letters to pitches is arbitrary and shows us little about the relationship among those pitches. From them we know that a series of As are the same pitch separated by octaves, but what is the relationship between an A and a B?[23] Also, while his "grid" and note names address discrete pitches beautifully, they fail to address the movement of those pitches through time, which we call rhythm. And even though musicians were certainly aware of rhythm and meter, theorists didn't tackle those elements for another century.

Remember earlier when I described notation's connection to words and its reliance on the syllable as the basic unit of music? When Guido labeled pitches, he was fixated on that first pillar—music's connection to words. As we move into the development of rhythmic notation, we approach the pillar of the syllable being foundational to that element of music. In the medieval Christian mind, each new syllable in a text had to begin on a different note. So, the question for musicians, especially as wordy new genres like the motet became popular, was how to group those syllables into a natural flow and communicate that flow to other musicians. Throughout the eleventh and twelfth centuries, musicians figured out how to differentiate between short and long syllables, but it wasn't until the late thirteenth century that a system for transcribing more complex rhythms came into practice. According to the English student studying at Notre Dame in Paris, who we only know as Anonymous IV, it was "the other Master Franco, from Cologne, who began to some extent to notate differently in their books."[24]

Franco of Cologne, a papal chaplain who seems to have studied in Paris and learned the latest French musical fashion, codified his new notational system in *Ars cantus mensurabilis* (*The Art of Measured Song*). His system was so popular that most manuscripts copied after his treatise use his "Franconian" system of notation. How does it work? Basically, Franco assigned three different shapes to three different note lengths: "The square with a tail is a long note (longa); the square without a tail is a short note (brevis); and a lozenge . . . is a 'semishort' note, a *semibrevis*."[25] Since we are still working in the medieval Christian mind, the relationship among these lengths is in threes—a "perfection" like the Holy Trinity of Father, Son, and Holy Spirit. This means that three semibreves equal a breve and three breves equal a long. Franco then went a step further by showing how to notate silence, the time in between musical sounds. He designated different lengths of vertical lines that, depending on how many staff lines they crossed, tell a musician how long to pause before proceeding.[26]

With these innovations of note names, a musical staff, and differing note shapes, we have the basis for our modern notational systems. And by considering what elements the names, staff, and shapes privilege by notating them accurately (namely melody, harmony, and rhythm), it's possible to see what the system does not deal with very well (namely, how to designate the balance of those elements and the desired sound color, musical features called texture and timbre). As musicians began to question the centrality of melody and harmony at the dawn of the twentieth century, they began to question a notation that worked for those elements but neglected the ones drawing their attention, and it is to that story that we now shift our attention

PUSHING AT THE BOUNDARIES

Even before the twentieth century, composers were already testing the limits of notation and pushing at its boundaries to articulate the sounds they imagined. Consider the final six measures of Franz Liszt's "Piano Sonata in B Minor." The pianist is busy intoning a series of treble-clef chords at a dynamic of *pp* when, in measure 755, Liszt asks the pianist to crescendo or increase the volume of an F-major triad on a four-beat tied note (see figure 4). This request is physically impossible on the piano, so why did Liszt notate it?[27] A clue comes in the following chord, a B major triad marked *ppp*. Liszt seems to have wanted to highlight the reduction in dynamics between the two chords. As a result, pianists must try and give a

sense of the dynamic shape the composer desired, often by offering a physical crescendo with their body since there cannot be a
musical crescendo.[28]

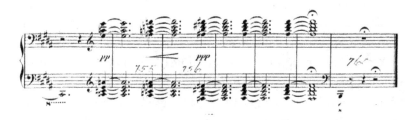

Figure 4. Franz Liszt, "Sonata in B Minor," (Leipzig: Breitkopf und Härtel, 1854),
mm. 754–760.

Composers and pianists like Liszt, frustrated with the strictures
of a pitch-centered notation, slowly began modifying notation,
some even going so far as to create a new type. The idea that there
are multiple types of notation may be new, but musicologists have
been trying to categorize notation for several decades.[29] I have
found Richard Rastall's formulation the most compelling and the
most useful for understanding the trajectory of modern notation
we are about to explore. He argued that most composers have one
of three purposes in mind for the notation they use: (1) mnemonic
notation (notation to remember something already learned by ear),
(2) sight-reading notation (notation to reproduce music immediately that has never been heard before), and (3) investigative notation (notation that requires study and rehearsal to reproduce the
music).[30] In this categorization, the neumes from St. Gall would be
mnemonic; notation employed over the past centuries in bands
and choirs, solos and ensembles would be sight-reading notation;
and the "Agnus Dei" from George Crumb's *Makrokosmos* would be
investigative.

As you have probably surmised, the twentieth century has been
a fascinating one for its musical experimentation as well as for its
changes to notational practice. Composers, turning their attention

to aspects of texture and timbre, also turned to investigative notation that required more study on the part of performers. They were able to explore investigative notation because of a shift in musical performance. In earlier centuries, music was often written quickly, rehearsed quickly, and then forgotten quickly after its performance. Patrons and audiences wanted a steady diet of new music and musicians responded. In the middle of the nineteenth century, musical practices and expectations gradually changed. Musicians began intensely practicing and rehearsing, and as a result, composers were able to demand more of performers. Instead of needing music that could be sight-read to a high level, musicians could take the time to investigate what the composer intended, leading to the situation I found in my early piano lessons where I was exhorted toward "fidelity to the score."[31] This culture of rehearsal has been a dominant one over the past two hundred years in Western Europe and the Americas, and we can track ever-increasing experimentation on top of ever-increasing rehearsal as we move closer to the present.

Let's start with some of the earliest changes to notation in the twentieth century. Arnold Schoenberg was a German composer who, in 1908, decided to abandon tonality's gravitational pull toward a single pitch and advocate the equality of all pitches. He called this approach "pantonality," but history records it as "atonality." Clearly Schoenberg was curious not only about new sounds but also new combinations of old sounds, and one of his most radical combinations was a style of singing he termed *Sprechstimme* from the German terms for "speech" and "voice." In Sprechstimme, the singer creates a sound halfway between speaking and singing—it has the color and exact pitches of singing but slides around the scale as we do when speaking. When Schoenberg went to notate this style first in *Gurrelieder* (1911) and then most famously in *Pierrot Lunaire* (1912), he had choices to make. He could have written prose instructions to the performer in the score but believed "that in musical notation one should express as little as possible with letters, or even words, and make ever-increasing use of signs (if possible pictures) which have nothing to do with letters."[32] What sign would most effectively tell the "Sprecher" to make the sound Schoenberg desired? He tried several different approaches, from an *X* replacing the note head to diamond-shaped note heads, before finally settling on placing an *X* across the stem of traditional notes (see figure 5).[33]

Figure 5. Arnold Schoenberg, *Pierrot Lunaire*, op. 21 (Vienna: Universal Edition, 1914). These are the first five measures of "Der kranke Mond."

Around the same time Schoenberg was grappling with how to notate *Sprechstimme*, a young boy in California began to write music using what he called "arm chords." In 1913, fifteen-year-old Henry Cowell wrote a piece of music called *Adventures in Harmony*, a "novelette" in six chapters whose third chapter asked pianists to play the entire bottom octave of the piano "with the whole hand," making gonging clusters that ring richly on the piano. He liked the sound so much that clusters became a foundational feature of Cowell's music through the 1920s and 1930s and occupied the final chapter of his important 1930 treatise *New Musical Resources*.[34] For Cowell, tone clusters were rooted in the overtone series and built by stacking major and minor seconds. In conventional notation, such a stack appears awkward on the staff, especially when it occupies an octave or more in the music, so by 1916, he was attempting to create a workable notation. Michael Hicks has helpfully charted Cowell's various solutions, starting with brackets and angles enclosing note heads to rounded beams or narrow bars stretching between the upper and lower pitches of the cluster (see figure 6).[35] In both of these cases, Cowell's clusters and Schoenberg's

Sprechstimme, the composers imagined the sounds they wanted and prodded notation to make it represent those sounds. Steeped in a tradition of sight-reading notation, they struggled to use that system, but since the notation they used was not concerned with the timbral variety they sought, the results were never completely satisfying. In the generation following their work, however that paradigm reversed, and composers abandoned sight-reading notation for investigative notation, as their new timbral ideas began creating space for innovation in composition.[36]

Figure 6. Henry Cowell, "The Hero Sun" (New York: Breitkopf Publications, 1922), mm. 4–8.

John Cage was at the vanguard of that next generation and found encouragement in his path when, in 1934, he enrolled in Cowell's course Primitive and Folk Origins of Music and perhaps attended the New Possibilities in Piano Playing class where Cowell demonstrated his cluster chords along with techniques for playing the strings of a piano.[37] After studying with Cowell, Cage moved home to California and began writing for percussion instruments because, as he later put it, "I believe that the use of noise to make music will continue and increase until we reach a music produced through the aid of electrical instruments which will make available for musical purpose any and all sounds that can be heard."[38] As you can imagine, Cage was fascinated with timbres that could not be captured by the notation available to him, and so he entered into a lifetime of exploring what is now called "graphic notation." He filled in the divots on a sheet of paper, he shaded rising and falling lines in different colors, and he even drew dots and lines on transparencies that could be laid one on top of another to create the score. Cage, as Alex Ross eloquently put it, "had an itch to try new things."[39]

The work with the transparencies was *Fontana Mix*, a composition for electronics derived from Cage's *Concert for Piano and Orchestra of 1958* (see figure 7). That larger score consists of sixty-three pages that can be played in any sequence, with any number of the pages, and any combination of piano, flute, clarinet, bassoon, trumpet, trombone, tuba, violins, violas, cello, and double bass. On those sixty-three pages are eighty-four "types" of composition and three sizes of notes that the performers interpret as either duration or amplitude or both. With the *Concert for Piano and Orchestra* (or the solos, duets, or chamber orchestral pieces it can be), Cage created a true investigative work that, while fully notated, "is no longer bound by a set of conventions assigning a specific meaning to each symbol, an ordered sequence of reading or even the necessity that the reading must be complete."[40]

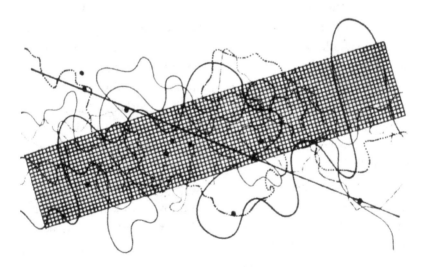

Figure 7. Fontana Mix by John Cage © Copyright 1958 by Henmar Press, Inc. All Rights Reserved.

We call Cage's notational approach in *Fontana Mix* "indeterminant" because it allows a given piece of music to be interpreted and performed in dramatically different ways. Cage ceded control of some aspects of the work to the performers, letting them choose their path while working within the larger structure he had created. What is perhaps most fascinating about this approach (at least for our discussion) is that indeterminant notation is one-way notation: you cannot reconstruct the notation from a given performance. With so much material left to the performer's discretion, you might be tempted to wonder if we should even call Cage the composer of the work. After all, the performers are, in some ways, equal with Cage in determining what we hear in performance. That we still label every performance of *Fontana Mix* as the work of Cage shows how music in this style privileges the composer's role over the performers. In other words, we are holding up the individual over the collective; we are reading investigative notation instead of mnemonic.

One of the main difficulties in this adoption of investigative notation is that it asks a lot of performers. Think through what response would be reasonable if you were presented with *Fontana Mix*. Take a few moments, look at the score, and then ask: Would you be excited? Nervous? Would you walk away in disgust or immediately sit down to try and figure out how it worked? Whatever the response, it is clear that by adopting investigative notation, composers were drastically changing the relationship between notation and the performer.

Throughout the 1950s, '60s, and '70s, composers asked performers to grapple with a veritable rainbow of notational options. Morton Feldman, a close compatriot of Cage's, created boxes within boxes in his *Projections* series,[41] giving duration in seconds, pitch ranges in the placement of boxes, and timbral instructions but not the precise notes and rhythms you are used to seeing in notation. Karlheinz Stockhausen, *l'enfant terrible*[42] of mid-century European music, increasingly used symbols in place of notes, such as his "plus-minus notation,"[43] where a performer picks an element of music and either increases or decreases it according to the corresponding mathematical symbol. Krzysztof Penderecki, a Polish originator of sonorism, or composing with texture, covered his score for "Threnody to the Victims of Hiroshima" (1960)[44] with an array of shapes, lines, and symbols in ten-second increments that asked performers to conjure new timbres from their string instruments. La Monte Young, one of the originators of the minimalist movement, began writing text-based scores with a series of works titled by their order within a given year. For example, "Composition 1960 #10"[45] reads, "Draw a straight line and follow it" while "Composition 1960 #13"[46] instructs, "The performer should prepare any composition and then perform it as well as he can." The following year, Yoko Ono, a multimedia artist associated with the New York City Fluxus group, created her "instruction painting" called "Voice Piece for Soprano"[47] in which she asks the performer to "scream. 1. against the wind 2. against the wall 3. against the sky." Cathy Berberian, one of the greatest interpreters of investigative notation, added her own spin on the style with "Stripsody," in which she notated musical sounds using onomatopoetic words taken from comic strips (see figure 8).

Figure 8. Stripsody by Cathy Berberian © Copyright 1966 by C.F. Peters Corporation. All Rights Reserved.

The movement toward investigative scores possibly reached its zenith with Cornelius Cardew's "Treatise" (1963–1967), a 193-page graphic score that demonstrates Cardew's experience as a graphic designer, with its beautiful and consistent symbology. The title "Treatise" refers to Ludwig Wittgenstein's *Tractatus*

Logico-Philosophicus, which attempted nothing less than finding the limitations of language in communicating reality. Virginia Anderson has pointed out, "Like Wittgenstein's search for the limits of language, Cardew was looking for a limit to the meaning of notation by using an arbitrary notation of symbols to which an eventual meaning would be assigned in performance."[48] Cardew created the ultimate indeterminant work by releasing "Treatise" with no performance instructions; performers are left to find their way through the score on their own, resulting in a startling array of exquisite realizations.

Still, even among all the wonderful realizations of "Treatise," there are some that do not seem to work, where the performers seem indifferent or confused or sardonic. It was this problem of performers not taking the notation seriously or taking liberties not allowed in the score that led many composers to abandon investigative notation and return to sight-reading notation toward the end of the century. Morton Feldman was one of the first composers to use graphic notation and one of the first to abandon the practice. Explaining his reasoning, he admitted that "if the performers sounded bad it was less because of their lapses of taste than because I was still involved with passages and continuity that allowed their presence to be felt."[49] In short, he wanted to exert more control over the sonic outcome of his music. Feldman knew that notation shaped music in the same way that language shaped thought, that it was not a secondary player in the creative process. But he was not happy with his notational options.[50] For their music to be performed by other musicians, composers like Feldman knew there had to be something written down, but was that notation the beginning of a dialogue between composer and performer or was it an end in and of itself?

WHERE DOES THE MUSIC RESIDE?

The conundrum Feldman presented leads to the end of my story and a few conclusions. From the previous section's survey, it seems as though there are two notational alternatives in the present day: notational anarchy (where composers create their own notational system) or slight additions and modifications to existing notation. I find that dichotomy less compelling as time goes by. As composers find a notation that works for their music, other composers seeking the same sound adopt that notation, and it slowly becomes standard. For the foreseeable future, we'll never completely move away from staff notation simply because it is so foundational to the musical culture it shaped. Think about all the ways people use notation today. Composers use it to remember ideas for later use, to communicate their ideas to performers, and to create publications. Performers use notation to learn a new piece of music, to refresh their memories on works they already know, and to perform all manner of music. Musicologists and theorists use notation to analyze music, attempting to discover how the music works and what connections it might have with other pieces of music. In other words, for some, notation and performance are generally understood to be equally essential in uncovering the essence of a musical work.[51]

Those two simple words, *musical work*, encapsulate the final value of so-called Western music that notation reveals. Remember my frustration at discovering that Chopin's music had multiple published versions? Having heard sermons about "fidelity to the score," I wanted what modern scholars call an "urtext" edition of Chopin. An urtext claims to be the earliest version of any text, and in the case of music, it often denotes an edition that presumes to contain the original text, without any editorial changes. The very idea of an urtext seems to propose that there is one perfect version of a piece of music, that the musical work exists outside of performance.

This idea of where a musical work resides is the final musical value given to us by Western notation, and it is the most recently adopted one. Think back to Hartker and the St. Gall manuscript. Some of the earliest notations musicologists have found in Western Europe were mnemonic. Music was an act of devotion, of communication, of reflecting God's glory back to God. It existed only in performance, and notation arose to make sure that monks remembered something they had already learned and experienced. Moving into the fifteenth through the eighteenth centuries, the relationship between notation and the music it captured flips. Notation is no longer a mnemonic of something already known but instead a sight-reading notation of music never heard before. Slowly, performance becomes secondary to the version of the music presented in the score, and a performer's job is to realize that score as precisely as possible. Or, another way to think of the "musical work" is that any performance is just one possible manifestation of a piece of music that exists in its most perfect form on the page. In fact, as Gavin Steingo has wryly observed, in today's world, "a work of music may exist that is *never* performed (as happens all too frequently in the lives of many young composers today)."[52] Yet even in these situations, we still refer to that score as a piece of music.[53]

If this concept seems a bit vague or confusing, perhaps one more example might help clarify this musical value. Consider Wolfgang Amadeus Mozart, the most-performed composer by US symphony orchestras in the 2012–2013 concert season, according to the League of American Orchestras.[54] When an orchestra performs Mozart's "Symphony No. 41 in C major, K. 551," their marketing materials proclaim, "The Kansas City Symphony performs Mozart's Symphony No. 41," and audiences expect to hear the work as it appears on most recordings. Compare that situation to "Yesterday" by the Beatles, one of the most recorded songs in modern history. When you buy/download/stream Frank Sinatra, The Supremes, Willie Nelson, Elvis, or even Bugs Bunny singing "Yesterday,"[55] you expect them to "cover" the song, to add their own personal interpretive stamp on the song. You talk about Sinatra's "Yesterday" as though the song exists apart from its original recording or any written version that happens to exist. Popular music does not venerate the "musical work" in the same way, perhaps because it is still a performance-based music rather than a notationally communicated one. In fact, if notated, popular music is usually written in a mnemonic fashion of melody and chord symbols that provide a guide to the music but do not provide the nuance of timbre or rhythmic groove.

Where does this leave us? We've seen that as it developed between the eighth and eleventh centuries, notation came to highlight certain musical elements and that those musical elements in turn became valued in certain musics. Melody, harmony, duration, and form are taught in undergraduate theory classes while timbre and texture lack the same level of systematic study. Similarly, because of our reliance on written music, we value the musical work apart from its performance. With these values foremost in our minds, let's return to our original questions: How does notation guide musical change? and, How does notation impact the way performers play a piece of music? It turns out that both Busoni and Partch were correct. Throughout history, notation and musical performance take turns leading each other. The earliest extant notation was a response to needs in performance, as monks needed to accurately recreate sacred music, but by the twentieth century, composers wanted new sounds and so pushed notation into new forms to communicate them. Similarly, there is a delicate dance between performers and the way notation shapes their performances based on the type of notation composers use. Mnemonic notation does little more than spur a performer's memory of the music; sight-reading notation provides clear guides to certain elements of music while leaving others open for interpretation; and investigative notation can be either extremely precise and controlling of performance or, as in the case of indeterminant notation, allow the performer more interpretive freedom within set boundaries. In answering both questions, it seems that notation exists to negotiate the relationship between, as Lydia Goehr has put it, "the abstract (the works) with the concrete (the performances)."[56]

Where will notation go from this point? It seems as though we are entering into a more conservative period in notational history, retreating from the more extreme examples of graphic notation yet incorporating some of those experiments into standard practice. Part of this notational stability is coming from composers creating a new "common practice" in composition. This common practice features more collaboration among musical styles, an increasing global outlook on the part of composers and performers, and the notion that all sound has musical potential.[57] But even more influential is notational software like Finale, Sibelius, MuseScore, and many others. The strictures of these software packages have made it more difficult to visualize and to realize elaborate graphic scores, and so composers don't attempt to create them. Some younger composers have returned to sight-reading notation because it is easier and they seem to feel that score and music are one and the same.

As for you creators, performers, listeners, teachers, and participants in music, with any luck thinking through some of the issues surrounding notation has accomplished the same magic that occurred that day long ago in my piano teacher's studio when I compared editions of Chopin's music. I hope that anyone reading this article will now look for the musical values inherent in musical systems, take what is useful from those values while questioning others, and forge a path toward a fulfilling engagement with music, a magic accomplished by cracking the code surrounding musical notation.

NOTES

1. See Jon Szanto, "The Legacy of Harry Partch," *Corporeal Meadows*, accessed September 12, 2020, http://www.corporealmeadows.com/.
2. See S. Andrew Granade, "'Some People Call Me the Space Cowboy': Sonic Markers of the Science Fiction Western," *Relocating the Sounds of the Western* (2019): 1–46; Samuel Andrew Granade, "Lifting the Veil: A Report on Graduate Music History Pedagogy Training in the United States (2015)," Journal of Music History Pedagogy 8, no. 2 (2018): 97–126.

3. Some of the musical terms used in this essay might be unfamiliar. Here is a handy glossary of musical terms you can consult if needed: https://wmich. edu/mus-gened/mus150/Glossary.pdf.

4. You can find Plato's allegory of the cave in *Republic*, VII, 514 a, 2 to 517 a, 7, or at this website: https://web.stanford.edu/class/ihum40/cave.pdf.

5. Fabio Álvarez, "Makrokosmos I with score, 1. Primeval Sounds (Genesis I) Cancer [Darkly mysterious] (Fabio Alvarez)," YouTube, May 12, 2020, https://www.youtube.com/watch?v=-8dobFjagSQ

6. See George N. Gianopoulos, "John Corigliano - Fantasia on an Ostinato for Piano (1985) [Score-Video]" YouTube, April 26, 2018, https://www.youtube.com/watch?v=PYlolvgo48E.

7. John Corigliano, *Fantasia on an Ostinato* (New York: G. Schirmer, 1987).

8. See Monoskop, "John Cage Notations 1969," Monoskop, accessed September 21, 2020, https://monoskop.org/File:Cage_John_Notations.pdf.

9. Ferruccio Busoni, *Sketch of a New Esthetic of Music*, trans. Theodore Baker (New York: G. Schirmer, 1911), 16.

10. Quarter tones are pitches halfway between our normal half steps in equal-temperament tuning—so a quarter tone exists between C and C-sharp, for instance. Composers including Béla Bartók Julián Carrillo, Alois Hába, Charles Ives, and Andrzej Milaszewski all experimented with quarter tones in the early twentieth century.

11. Harry Partch, *Genesis of a Music*, 2nd ed. (New York: Da Capo Press, 1974), 356.

12. Morton Feldman, "Crippled Symmetry," in B. H. Friedman, ed., *Give My Regards to Eighth Street: Collected Writings of Morton Feldman* (Cambridge, MA: Exact Change, 2000), 143.

13. John Sloboda, *Exploring the Musical Mind: Cognition, Emotion, Ability, Function* (Oxford: Oxford University Press, 2005), 7–11.

14. See U-M Library Online Exhibits, "What Is an Antiphonary?" Regents of the University of Michigan, accessed September 12, 2020, https://apps.lib. umich.edu/online-exhibits/exhibits/show/singing-the-antiphonary--mich-/the-manuscript.

15. See Gustav Scherrer, "Antiphonarium officii (Antiphonary for liturgy of the hours)," (Switzerland: Stiftsbibliothek, 1875), https://www.e-codices.unifr.ch/en/list/one/csg/0390.

16. Leo Treitler, "What Kind of Thing Is Musical Notation," in *Reflections on Musical Meaning and Its Representations* (Bloomington: Indiana University Press, 2011), 108.

17. Thomas Forrest Kelly, *Capturing Music: The Story of Notation* (New York: W. W. Norton, 2015), 12.

18. Guido, quoted in Dolores Pesce, "Guido d'Arizzo, Ut queant laxis, and Musical Understanding," in *Music Education in the Middle Ages and the Renaissance*, ed. Russell E. Murray Jr., Susan Forcher Weiss, and Cynthia J. Cyrus (Bloomington: Indiana University Press, 2010), 26.

19. Guido, quoted in Oliver Strunk, *Source Readings in Music History*, rev. ed., ed. Leo Treitler (New York, W. W. Norton, 1998), 212–13.

20. John Haines, "The Origins of the Musical Staff," *Musical Quarterly* 91, no. 3/4 (Fall–Winter 2008): 331.

21. Richard Rastal, *The Notation of Western Music: An Introduction* (London: J. M. Dent, 1983), 128–31.

22. Why didn't Guido have "Ti" in his system? His system was moveable, so he would shift the "Ut" to get the notes he needed. As Thomas Kelly points out, "Guido was preeminently a teacher: he wanted people to be able to learn to sing, and to sing accurately, with the least amount of trouble and the greatest possible accuracy." Thomas Forrest Kelly, *Capturing Music: The Story of Notation* (New York: W. W. Norton, 2015), 70. In other words, "Movable Do" preceded "fixed Do" in music education.

23. Leo Treitler, "What Kind of Thing Is Musical Notation," in *Reflections on Musical Meaning and Its Representations* (Bloomington: Indiana University Press, 2011), 112.

24. Anonymous IV, quoted in Edward H. Roesner, "Who 'Made' the 'Magnus Liber'?" *Early Music History* 20 (2001): 228.

25. Thomas Forrest Kelly, *Capturing Music: The Story of Notation* (New York: W. W. Norton, 2015), 126.

26. Richard Rastal, *The Notation of Western Music: An Introduction* (London: J. M. Dent, 1983), 47–56.

27. If these kinds of notational oddities are intriguing, visit http://html.sice.indiana.edu/~donbyrd/CMNExtremesBody.htm for a compendium of extremes of notation.

28. In this recording, accessible at https://youtu.be/hq7xiok7nZU?t=1654, pianist Yulianna Avdeeva has a fascinating solution to this problem: she raises her head and looks upward to signal the crescendo, closing her eyes and bowing her head for the return to the original dynamic. The sound does not change, but see if you have an emotional response to her gesture.

29. Musicologist Charles Seeger first identified two types of notation in 1958, and the names he coined remain in use. See Charles Seeger, "Prescriptive and Descriptive Music-Writing." *Musical Quarterly* 44, no. 2 (April 1958): 184–95. Seeger used the term "descriptive notation" to refer to notation that attempts to show the sound of a musical work to the level that you

can identify previously unknown music with it while "prescriptive notation" was where a composer told the performer how to produce a sound. Music before the twentieth century mainly was of the descriptive variety—staff notation as learned in first-year theory courses is largely two-dimensional, listing the melody, harmony, rhythm, dynamics, and instrumentation of a piece of music. Think of descriptive notation as a visual recording of a piece of music. As composers began to stretch the sounds that were possible on instruments and the types of sounds that could be considered "music," they moved to prescriptive notation where they tell how to make the music. In this case, you can consider the notation an IKEA instruction manual to study and follow to realize the music even as it seems confusing at times. Meiko Kanno, "Prescriptive Notation: Limits and Challenges," *Contemporary Music Review* 26, no. 2 (April 2007): 232–35.

30. Richard Rastall, *The Notation of Western Music: An Introduction* (London: J. M. Dent, 1983), 257.

31. Rastall, *The Notation of Western Music*, 257.

32. Arnold Schoenberg, *Style and Idea*, ed. Leonard Stein, trans. Leo Black (Berkeley: University of California Press, 1984), 351.

33. Because Schoenberg was asking the performer to make sounds not found in the notational system, performers have constantly questioned what Schoenberg wanted for the exact timbre. See Aidan Soder, "Sprechstimme," in Arnold Schoenberg, *Pierrot Lunaire: A Study of Vocal Performance Practice* (Lewiston, NY: Edwin Mellen Press, 2008), 10–19.

34. Henry Cowell, *New Musical Resources*, with David Nicholls (Cambridge: Cambridge University Press, 1996), 117–144.

35. Michael Hicks, "Cowell's Clusters," *Musical Quarterly* 77, no. 3 (1993): 442–44.

36. Elena Dubinets, "American Music from the Second Half of the 20th Century: Notation and Compositional Techniques," *21st Century Music* 11, no. 8 (2004): 1.

37. Leta E. Miller, "Henry Cowell and John Cage: Intersections and Influences, 1933–1941," *Journal of the American Musicological Society* 59, no. 1 (Spring 2006): 52–53. Miller helpfully shows how Cowell influenced many aspects of Cage's work through the 1930s to the 1950s, including "recording technology, percussion, dance, performance indeterminacy, sliding tones, extended instrumental techniques, and formal structures based on rhythmic organization."

38. John Cage, *Silence* (Hanover, NH: Wesleyan University Press, 1961), 3–4.

39. Alex Ross, "Searching for Silence" *New Yorker*, October 4, 2010, https://www.newyorker.com/magazine/2010/10/04/searching-for-silence.)

40. Christopher Fox, "Opening Offer or Contractual Obligation? On the

Prescriptive Function of Notation in Music Today," *Tempo* 68, no. 269 (2014): 9–10.

41. See A Year from Monday, "Reading Through John Cage's Writings, 2011–2012," A Year from Monday, accessed September 12, 2020, http://www.ayear-frommonday.com/.

42. See Grammarist, "Enfant terrible," Grammarist, accessed September 12, 2020, https://grammarist.com/idiom/enfant-terrible/.

43. Stockhausenspace, *Stockhausen: Sounds in Space* (blog), Stockhausenspace, accessed September 12, 2020, http://stockhausenspace.blogspot.com/2015/06/plus-minus.html.

44. Music History Collaborative Blog, *The Graphic Notation of Krzysztof Penderecki's* "Threnody for the Victims of Hiroshima," Music History Collaborative Blog, April 6, 2015, https://musichistoryfsu.wordpress.com/2015/04/06/the-graphic-notation-of-krzysztof-pendereckis-threnody-for-the-victims-of-hiroshima/.

45. Jennifer Gersten, "You Have to See These Unusual Performances of La Monte Young's 'Compositions 1960,'" Q2 Music, April 24, 2017, https://www.wqxr.org/story/you-have-see-these-unsual-performances-la-monte-youngs-compositions-1960/.

46. MoMA, "La Monte Young Composition 1960 #13 to Richard Huelsenbeck and Composition 1960 #15 to Richard Huelsenbeck 1960," Art and Artists, accessed September 12, 2020, https://www.moma.org/collection/works/127640?artist_id=6520&locale=en&page=1&sov_refer-rer=artist.

47. Andrew Russeth, "Yoko Ono, Voice Piece for Soprano, 1961," Museum of Modern Art, New York, April 28, 2007, https://www.flickr.com/photos/sixteen-miles/4747195485.

48. Virginia Anderson, "'Well, It's a Vertebrate . . .': Performer Choice in Cardew's *Treatise," Journal of Musicological Research* 25, nos. 3–4 (December 2006): 292. Anyone interested in flipping through Cardew's score can find it digitally here: http://davidhall.io/treatise-score-graphic-notation/.

49. Feldman, quoted in Brett Boutwell, "'The Breathing of Sound Itself': Notation and Temporality in Feldman's Music to 1970," *Contemporary Music Review* 32, no. 6 (2013): 536.

50. Brett Boutwell, "'The Breathing of Sound Itself': Notation and Temporality in Feldman's Music to 1970," *Contemporary Music Review* 32, no. 6 (2013): 532.

51. Meiko Kanno, "Prescriptive Notation: Limits and Challenges," *Contemporary Music Review* 26, no. 2 (April 2007): 231.

52. Gavin Steingo, "The Musical Work Reconsidered, In Hindsight" *Current Musicology* 97 (Spring 2014): 82–83.

53. If this idea seems fascinating, I'd suggest reading Christopher Small's work, where he proposes adding the word "musicking" to English, saying that "to music is to take part, in any capacity, in a musical performance, whether by performing, by listening, by rehearsing or practicing, by providing material for performance (what is called composing), or by dancing." Christopher Small, *Musicking: The Meanings of Performing and Listening* (Hanover, NH: University Press of New England, 1998), 9.

54. For statistics on performance, see the League of American Orchestras, *ORR 13 Summary Report* (New York: LAO, 2012–2013), http://www.americanorchestras.org/images/stories/ORR_1213/ORR13%20summary%20report.pdf.

55. Gamer Zylo, "Bugs & Friends—Yesterday," YouTube, June 14, 2008, https://www.youtube.com/watch?v=1XjU6unPIDo.

56. Lydia Goehr, *The Imaginary Museum of Musical Works: An Essay in the Philosophy of Music*, 2nd ed. (Oxford: Oxford University Press, 2007), 231.

57. Composer and scholar Robert Carl is wonderfully prescient about the future direction of music in his "Eight Waves a Composer will Ride in this Century," NewMusicBox, June 1, 2013, https://nmbx.newmusicusa.org/eight-waves-a-composer-will-ride-in-this-century/.

ANCIENT MESOPOTAMIAN MUSIC, THE POLITICS OF RECONSTRUCTION, AND EXTREME EARLY MUSIC

Samuel Dorf

I write this piece primarily as a musicologist and amateur early music practitioner (viola da gamba player) who tries to understand the ways twentieth- and twenty-first century musicians and scholars have imagined and performed ancient music and dance. This essay emerged from my book project Performing Antiquity: Ancient Greek Music and Dance from Paris to Delphi, 1890-1935[1] *and brings my training as a historical musicologist and dance historian to bear on issues typically of concern to archaeologists, classicists, and linguists.*

While working on that book, I kept running across a number of individuals working now who are deeply engaged in the same kinds of reconstruction and performance projects like the ones I discuss. This essay serves as the first step toward a "sequel" so to speak to my previous book. I started by interviewing a number of these practitioners of extreme early music (music from before 800 CE), including performers, instrument builders, and scholars in classics and archaeology. Their generosity of time and willingness to share inform my gentle treatment of their work.

I am not here to serve as judge and jury to determine if their interpreta-
tions, recreations, restorations, or composition are authentic, and I hope
that readers don't get too caught up in these questions either. Instead, I
hope readers use the politics and performance of extreme early music to
interrogate the ways we perform multiple pasts today.

———————————

Sometime in July 2015, Daesh (al-Dawla al-Islamiya fil Iraq wa al-Sham, the self-proclaimed Islamic State or ISIS) apprehended Khaled al-Asaad,[2] the chief archaeologist in charge of preserving the United Nations Educational, Scientific and Cultural Organization (UNESCO) World Heritage site in Palmyra, Syria.[3] After a month of interrogations and presumed torture, al-Asaad refused to reveal where the site's most prized relics were hidden, and on August 18, 2015, al-Asaad was publicly beheaded in the city square near the ancient Palmyra arch. A few months later, Daesh blew up the eighteen-hundred-year-old ancient Roman Arch of Triumph in Palmyra.[4] Daesh's motivations for destroying and stealing cultural artifacts are multiple[5]: cultural heritage artifacts are valuable on the black market, and razing the sites plays a role in the group's historical and theological mission.

The loss of the arch elicited worldwide condemnation followed by almost immediate calls to reconstruct the Roman ruins to their former ruined glory. And so in April 2016, in collaboration with an international team of researchers and artisans, Oxford's Institute for Digital Archaeology[6] unveiled a reconstruction of the famed arch in London's Trafalgar Square. The artists and researchers produced a nearly identical stand-in for the toppled arch not merely as an exercise in craftsmanship or archaeological reconstruction, but to send a very public message to ISIS that history cannot be destroyed forever and that the world will come together to rebuild it. The ceremony in front of the draped arch was widely attended and combined speeches from elected officials and members of the reconstruction team as well as a performance of music sung in ancient Babylonian—a language of the ancient Mesopotamian cultures that thrived in the lands of modern-day Iraq and Syria in the first millennium BCE. The keynote was delivered by then mayor of London, Boris Johnson, who proclaimed, "We are here in the spirit of defiance, defiance of the barbarians who destroyed the original of this arch as they destroyed the original of so many monuments and relics in Syria and in the Middle East and in Palmyra." His speech ended with a shout-out to the team that reconstructed the arch. "Congratulations to the Institute for Digital Archaeology," he yelled to the crowd. "How many digits do you think Daesh deserve? I think two fingers [a vulgar gesture akin to the middle finger in the United States and Canada] to Daesh from the Institute of [*sic*, for Digital] Archaeology and from London folks."[7] See figure 1.

Figure 1. Mayor of London Boris Johnson gives Daesh two digits in front of the reconstructed Palmyra Arch, April 2016.

At the conclusion of his robust attack on Daesh, Johnson called for his staff to unveil the Roman arch—itself a symbol of imperialist victory over an ancient Middle Eastern people—for all of

London to see. As the mayor posed for a few pictures, singer/composer Stef Conner and harpists Mark Hamer and Andy Lowings stepped forward to perform the title track from their 2014 album *The Flood* (see figure 2).[8] Their chosen piece was a new setting of a section from the four-thousand-year-old tale *The Epic of Gilgamesh*. Harpist Hamer accompanied Conner's voice on a playable reconstruction of the forty-five-hundred-year-old lyre of Ur, itself based upon an original destroyed in the looting following the US invasion of Baghdad in the second Iraq War.[9]

Figure 2. Boris Johnson and Stef Conner in front of the reconstructed Palmyra Arch, April 2016.

Within this one performance we have a variety of reconstructions. There are material reconstructions (the arch and the harp) and performed reconstructions of ancient texts with new melodies (Conner's newly composed song), and all three adhere to different expectations of historical accuracy and fidelity. Most importantly, although based upon scholarly sources, the arch, the harp, and the song reconstructions are not meant for a strictly scholarly audience but rather serve as public exemplars of what has been lost and saved from ancient Mesopotamian cultures. Mixed together, the material and the performance reinforce each other's authenticity. In this essay, I explore the power and connections between performed and material reconstructions of what I am calling *extreme early music*, an approach to early music performance that privileges experimental practice as well as techniques and methods from anthropology and archaeology. When antiquity appears as both material and live reconstruction, the allure of the material often gives the performance a sheen of archaeological authenticity the performers perhaps never intended to have. I intend to explore some of the methods and politics of material and performance reconstruction before looking at Conner's setting of the Gilgamesh narrative. I draw on recent scholarship in archaeological preservation and conservation as well as performance studies to contextualize and analyze Conner's music in ancient Mesopotamian languages and the reconstruction and performance of Mesopotamian lyres. The multiple reconstructions of Eastern Mediterranean culture discussed here not only provide a setting to test the limits of musical reconstructions, refabrications, and reinventions but also demonstrate ways musical reconstructions function as a form of history for general audiences. Such public performances, I argue, sidestep scholarly questions of authenticity and allow us to see how, when, and to whom scholarship becomes "real."

OWNERSHIP, COLONIALISM, AND CULTURAL APPROPRIATION

Who owns antiquity? Museums and nation-states have been arguing over cultural artifacts from antiquity for centuries. Famous examples include the so-called Elgin Marbles removed from the Parthenon in Athens in the first decade of the nineteenth century and shipped to London where they are now on display in the British Museum,[10] and the more recent purchase of stolen Iraqi antiquities by representatives of Hobby Lobby who were forced to return the objects in 2018.[11] When it comes to concrete antiquities—physical objects—who has the right to the materials? Does the modern Greek government "own" ancient Hellenic artifacts adorning ruins or buried in the ground centuries before modern Greece became a nation-state? Do the colonialist powers that acquired them (through payment and/or theft) deserve the right to provide continued care and protection to these artifacts?

James Cuno, a curator and art historian, makes the argument that ancient cultural property does not necessarily belong to the modern nations where that property is found.

> What is the relationship between, say, modern Egypt and the antiquities that were part of the land's Pharaonic past? The people of modern-day Cairo do not speak the language of the ancient Egyptians, do not practice their religion, do not make their art, wear their dress, eat their food, or play their music, and they do not adhere to the same kinds of laws or form of government the ancient Egyptians did. All that can be said is that they occupy the same (actually less) stretch of the earth's geography.[12]

Cuno, borrowing terms from legal scholar John Henry Merryman, stresses preservation of cultural objects using rigorous means to seek truth about our past in these objects and providing the greatest access to objects for scholars and a global public.[13] All of these arguments, however, gloss over the fact that these objects often have real economic value and that concentrating the preservation of, access to, and "truth" of antiquities in the cities of the world's most powerful countries (i.e., London, Chicago, Berlin, New York City, etc.) hurts the communities from whence these materials come.[14]

These material objects from the past are also part of how nations tell their stories. In his examination of imperialism and colonialism in Western literature and culture, Edward Said defines imperialism as "the practice, the theory, and the attitudes of a dominating metropolitan center ruling a distant territory."[15] Imperialism envelopes both the colonized people and the colonizing power in profound ways, leading Said to note that "nations themselves *are* narrations. The power to narrate, or to block other narratives from forming and emerging, is very important to culture and imperialism, and constitutes one of the main connections between them."[16] Therefore, those who "own" antiquity narrate antiquity. However, those who "perform" antiquity can also "own" antiquity and they, too, have the power to narrate, or block, emerging narratives of antiquity from coming forth. Perhaps none of these issues matters as much as looming questions of who has the right to reconstruct ruins (material and performed).

AUTHENTICITY AND MATERIAL RECONSTRUCTION: HARPS AND ARCHES

One of the founders of modern archaeology, British archaeologist Sir Charles Leonard Woolley, discovered a set of four ancient lyres in his 1929 excavations of the Mesopotamian city of Ur—the birthplace of the biblical Abraham and of Western monotheism. His expeditions to territories in the Middle East under British colonial rule helped popularize the science of archaeology and also reinforced colonialist ideas of ancient Mesopotamia.[17] Although the wooden frames of the forty-five-hundred-year-old instruments had disintegrated, the metal and jeweled decorations remained. See figure 3.

Woolley used plaster casts to preserve the shape of the lyres' frames and artisans reconstructed the lyres before placing the precious metals back onto the reconstructed frame. Woolley's team then distributed the reconstructed instruments to various institutions that helped in the excavation: two are at the British Museum,[18] one is at the University of Pennsylvania's Museum of Archaeology and Anthropology,[19] and the great Golden Lyre of Ur (also known as the Great Bull Lyre) ended up at the National Museum of Iraq in Baghdad where it stood on display until the

Figure 3. Lyres of Ur buried in a tomb.

US-led invasion of Iraq in 2003. In early April of 2003, the museum was looted. The lyre went missing, only to be found in pieces. The irreparably damaged gold and mother-of-pearl bull's head was subsequently discovered in the flooded basement vaults of Iraq's Central Bank. Looters stripped parts of the body of much of its gold and left the remains in a parking lot.[20] In figure 4, one can see the instrument stripped of its gold and in pieces. The sound box is on the left, the crossbar in the middle, and the two arms on the right.

The loss and destruction of antiquities like the lyre in the fallout of the invasion of Iraq brought wide, international condemnation. It also spurred many not merely to lament and protect the remaining treasures but also to reconstruct as a form of retaliation.[21] Andy Lowings,[22] who reconstructed the lyre of Ur, is a British civil engineer who has overseen massive projects in Dubai and played a key role in the development of the Channel Tunnel: he is not an archaeologist or Assyriologist. He is, however, an amateur harpist[23] with an interest in the culture of the Middle East.

Figure 4. A badly damaged lyre of Ur.

Ancient instruments had been reconstructed before, but Lowings sought to reproduce the work as both an art object as well as a functional musical instrument able to reperform the lost sounds of a twice-destroyed culture. Begun in 2003 during the Iraq War, Lowings's reconstruction work spared no expense in the quest for fidelity to the original instrument's qualities: Iraqi cedar wood was smuggled out of a war zone to build its frame; the instrument is studded with lapis lazuli and other precious jewels and stones; the frame is covered in nearly a kilogram of pure 24 karat gold (at the time worth about $13,000 alone). Furthermore, Lowings used historical materials and methods to create the instrument and took cues from other harp-playing traditions that he was familiar with from across the Middle East and East Africa, where similarly styled lyres are still played. For example, since none of the strings or tuning winches survived, Lowings had to surmise how many strings to include, what material to use, and determine their gauge and length. He noted that the soundboard of the instrument had eight lapis lazuli emblems, which he then inferred to indicate eight strings. He chose gut as a string material although other materials (cloth, metal, hide) may have worked as well. His strings run up from a bridge to a top bar where they are secured and tuned using cloth and wooden pegs (a combination of ancient Egyptian and modern tuning peg technology). These decisions were all made through a combination of archaeological study, the study of world harp traditions, and experimental practice.[24]

THE POLITICS OF MATERIAL RECONSTRUCTION

Both Lowings and the creator of the recreated Palmyra arch Roger Michel emphasize the ability of material culture to help US and European publics connect to the past. In a talk delivered at the Library of Congress in 2009,[25] note the ways Lowings tries to appeal to a "universal" historical, religious, and cultural legacy as a way to avoid potential criticism for his reconstruction of the lyre of Ur: "This is an instrument from before everything . . . from before Christianity, from before Judaism. This is an instrument that connects us all and so nobody can have any fault with us bringing it alive and to today, and to show the history of those ancient times." Lowings refers not only to the material construction but more importantly to its performative potential to connect modern audiences to an imagined ancient Judeo-Christian musical ur-source (or "Ur"-source).[26]

Similarly fascinated with how the public engages with his reconstructions, Michel, the director of the Palmyra project said on NPR's *Weekend Edition*[27] about the controversaries surrounding digital reconstructions: "In the West, we are very fetishistic about originality. We want to touch the object that the master touched. . . . For people in other parts of the world, the role of objects is not to somehow through the object itself bring you close to history. It is a visual cue that provides memories of history. The history and heritage resides in the mind."[28] Michel has also been far more explicit in discussing the ways conflict and war have driven his work. "My intention," he declared in a *Guardian* interview, "is to show Islamic State that anything they can blow up we can rebuild exactly as it was before, and rebuild it again and again. We will use technology to disempower Isis [*sic*]."²⁹ His statements could imply that a key element of this reconstruction project was an attempt to possess an ancient symbol of ancient European imperialism and to stage it across the world as a modern symbol of Western culture and power.

The economics of these projects prove complicated and rife with controversy as well. Tim Williams, in a series of editorials for the journal *Conservation and Management of Archaeological Sites*, has lamented the cost and questioned the ethics of reconstructing these items: "So the question remains, is this where resources are best spent? Of course humanitarian aid comes first, but the relatively meagre resources for heritage conservation and restoration can be monies well spent—vital to a sustainable tourism industry, lifeblood for the rebuilding of the Syrian economy. But rebuilding facsimiles, however good, of the ruins of Palmyra: the question must be why?"³⁰ Sultan Barakat's analysis of best-practice policies for postwar reconstruction and recovery of cultural heritage places an emphasis less on external actors and more on local communities; in practice, that means developing a shared comprehensive vision for postwar recovery of cultural heritage.³¹ Postwar reconstruction, Barakat argues, is "a range of holistic activities in an integrated process designed not only to reactivate economic and social development but at the same time to create a peaceful environment that will prevent a relapse into violence."³² It would be hard to argue that the Trafalgar Square performance or any of the subsequent erections of the arch in cities such as New York City, Dubai, Florence, Arona, and most recently Washington, DC, accomplish Barakat's goals.³³ What local people wish to preserve and how they wish to preserve it after war is often different from the aims and methods of international actors. Or, as Layton and Thomas write, "Not all societies use the remains of the past as a means of substantiating their identity."[34] Furthermore, restoring the arch of Palmyra cannot undo or ever adequately respond to the gruesome murder of Khaled al-Asaad. Material reconstruction is not without its complications.

Others involved in reconstruction have expressed similar motivations. In an interview with CBS Evening News, Italian politician and former mayor of Rome Francesco Rutelli described his own interests in the reconstruction of cultural artifacts: "We want to demonstrate that the reconstructions and the scientific terms of reference is [sic] necessary and possible." When the interviewer remarked that reconstruction is not the same as bringing back the original, Rutelli replied, "Absolutely not, but we can't accept that the last word is the word of terrorists."[35]

MUSICAL RECONSTRUCTIONS: "THE FLOOD" AND EXTREME EARLY MUSIC

Michel's and Lowings's work in material reconstruction fixates on the details of fidelity to the original object, but in their display, the arch and lyre are more like performed reconstructions in that the spaces and contexts of their public display seek to frame the ways we think of that past in the present. If these material reconstructions produce physical emblems that simultaneously connect publics to ancient pasts and fight terrorism, what might the nonphysical reconstructions of these cultures accomplish for audiences? Just as Michel's arch of Palmyra is meant to be touched, Lowings's lyre was built to be touched and played, not to sit in a museum under glass. After he founded the Lyre of Ur Project as a nonprofit in 2003, he spent many years building the instrument. He did not meet composer and singer Stef Conner until 2012.[36] Lowings found Conner through an informal network of individuals interested in ancient harps—what Conner affectionately calls the "old lyre gang."[37] Lowings initially emailed her with an invitation to collaborate on what he called "very early music."[38]

What Lowings asked Conner to do wasn't *just* early music, but rather *extreme* early music. Scholarship concerning the performance of early music and the historically informed performance (HIP) movement are usually limited to notated European music traditions ranging from the thousand-year period, from 800 to 1800 CE, with the most activity concerning music from the two-hundred-and-fifty-year period of 1500 to 1750. Traditional narratives of music history and historical performance practice often skim over the earliest traces of human music making from prehistory to the middle ages, because scholars often assume that there isn't enough material to properly reconstruct the music of the earliest human civilizations.[39] That assumption is predicated on the idea that in order to properly or authentically reconstruct ancient music we need to rely on ancient sources alone.[40] A number of scholars and performer-scholars are seeking to rectify performance and scholarly lacunae by reimagining and performing music based upon reconstructed ancient sources, often using novel performance techniques and styles.

Reimagination, performance, discovery, and reconstruction play to our interest in "being there," in experiencing the past anew. Like living history projects and battle reenactments, the performance of a reconstruction may create, in the public, a sense of being there, or of time collapsing. In her study of Civil War reenactors, Rebecca Schneider writes that many reenactors feel that "if they repeat an event *just so*, getting the details as close as possible to fidelity, they will have touched time and time will have recurred."[41] The comparison to Civil War reenactors also highlights the high stakes of their performances. Reenactors are invested in their performances in ways that traditional stage actors and musicians might not be. As Schneider[42] has written, however, it is not just about touching time: "[Reenactors] also engage in this activity as a way of accessing what they feel the documentary evidence upon which they rely misses—that is, live experience. Many [Civil War reenactors] fight not only to 'get it right' as it *was* but to get it right as it *will be* in the future of the archive to which they see themselves contributing."[43]

Schneider's argument here is quite similar to Richard Taruskin's in his influential essay "The Pastness of the Present and the Presence of the Past." In this critique of the early music movement of the twentieth century, Richard Taruskin makes a distinction between the "authentistic" and "authentic" performance: "The former construes intentions 'internally,' that is, in spiritual, metaphysical, or emotional terms, and sees their realization in terms of the 'effect' of a performance, while the latter construes intentions in terms of empirically ascertainable—and hence, though tacitly, external—facts, and sees their realization purely in terms of sound."[44] That is, Taruskin sees a difference between those in the early music movement who seek to tell history as they really like/feel it and those who tell it as it really was. Responding to the explosion of creative approaches to performing music of the past that began in the 1950s and '60s with the work of Noah Greenberg, Paul Hilliard, and David Munrow, Taruskin offers a way out of the performative problems of "authenticity." Due to countless factors, performers of early music cannot recreate musical performances how they really were, but rather "their job is to discover, if they are lucky, *wie es eigentlich uns gefällt*—how we really like it,"[45] and that can draw upon a number of authenticities. A composer's intentions are both unknowable and not always ideal guides to authentic performance. Or, as Tarsukin writes, "everyone claims it."[46] In this telling, those who claim specialized knowledge about the way Johann Sebastian Bach might have performed his keyboard suites could no longer criticize the pianist who played the works on modern instruments. Taruskin also urges listeners to not use historical facts and religious adherence to texts "as a veritable stick to beat modern performers."[47] However, while he argues against beating up modern performers for adding personal choice and inspiration to their performances, he still highly values those historical tools used as weapons by his critics: "Original instruments, historical treatises, and all the rest have proven their value," he concludes.[48] Taruskin's historicization of authenticity seemed to put the matter to bed for musicologists in the 1990s, and Schneider's contributions to performance studies have greatly impacted the conversations within that discipline. When applied to extreme early music, especially in the cases of musical cultures where far fewer materials exist, musical "authenticity" that relies on an adherence to a composer's intensions, original instruments, and historical treatises is impossible: there just isn't enough information. That said, Taruskin's work around this problem privileges at least a conversation among those historical sources, performing traditions, and the living performer. For extreme early music, there are no remaining traditions, and the sources are so few that it is impossible to have the kind of engagement that Taruskin seems to call for.

Conner herself makes no claim to the type of authenticity lambasted by Taruskin in her music for *The Flood*. The title track of the album and the song that Conner and Lowings performed under the arch of Palmyra in Trafalgar Square, called "The Flood," is an excerpt from the ancient story *The Epic of Gilgamesh*—a tale of "human mortality as a consequence of divine selfishness."[49] The story opens with the great king Gilgamesh mistreating his subjects in the walled city of Uruk. The gods punish him by creating a wild man, Enkidu, to stop the king. However, Enkidu and Gilgamesh become best friends and go on adventures together until Enkidu is killed, leaving Gilgamesh devastated.

Confronted with the death of his best friend and his own mortality, Gilgamesh sets forth on a futile journey to find everlasting life. He seeks Utnapishtim, one of the few remaining survivors of the great flood. Upon meeting him, Gilgamesh tells of the loss of his friend, Enkidu, and his fear of death. "I would not give him up for burial, / Until a worm fell out of his nose. / I was frightened. . . . / My friend whom I loved is turned into clay, / Enkidu, my friend whom I loved, is turned into clay! / Shall I too not lie down like him, / And never get up, forever and ever?"[50] Confronted with Gilgamesh's tale of woe, Utnapishtim chides the king for his self-pity. How dare he, Gilgamesh, think that his life is worthy of eternity:

> How long does a building stand before it falls?
> How long does a contract last? How long will brothers
>
> share the inheritance before they quarrel?
> How long does hatred, for that matter, last?
>
> Time after time the river has risen and flooded.
> The insect leaves the cocoon to live but a minute.
>
> How long is the eye able to look at the sun?
> From the very beginning nothing at all has lasted.[51]

The Epic of Gilgamesh suggests that even our most enduring monuments last but a moment in the grand scheme of cosmic history, each just another futile attempt at everlasting life. Why, then, do we reconstruct and reperform when death, violence, decay, and memory no longer connect us to the long-dead culture we wish to resurrect?

THE DANGEROUS ALLURE OF RECONSTRUCTION

As sung by Conner under the reconstructed Palmyra arch, the flood narrative of Tablet XI in *The Epic of Gilgamesh* becomes more than just a story of destruction and survival. It becomes a metaphor for the historical enterprise writ large. Gilgamesh's arduous journey leads him to Utnapishtim, "the Distant One,"[52] to learn the secret of cheating death, of everlasting life. The old man's speech begins: "I will reveal to you, O Gilgamesh, a secret matter, / And a mystery of the gods I will tell you."[53] It is the dream of many historians: to find the sole surviving informant, the last narrative account of the great secret. It is the search for everlasting life many scholars seek in publishing their work. The ability to check or confirm, to see if they got it *right*: if the reproduced ancient lyre sounds like the *real* one did thousands of years ago; if our performance of Bach sounds at all like Bach's performance of Bach. Reconstruction provides this illusion, and it is doubly dangerous to see present and past works, material and performed, merge. As Vanessa Agnew describes, "With its vivid spectacles and straightforward narratives, reenactment apparently fulfills the failed promise of academic history—knowledge entertainingly and authoritatively presented."[54] Reenactment sells: the desire to see the past as we imagine it tends to trump our rational ability to recognize that what we are hearing is really modern. It is a cumbersome cognitive hurdle to leap over. Seeing the ancient instrument makes one hear ancient music regardless of when that music was first created or performed.

The flood narrative in Conner's song begins after Utnapishtim has loaded the boat with all types of animals, his family, his possessions, and craftsmen. He caulks the door shut, and then the deluge begins. Dark clouds descend, the gods destroy the earth, dikes overflow, the whole earth is set ablaze, light turns to darkness, the earth is smashed like a clay pot. The destruction is so fierce that the terrified gods cower like dogs and Ishtar—the goddess of sex, love, fertility, war, and combat—sees the destruction of humanity and screams "like a woman in childbirth"[55] (a sonic effect heard in Conner's performance).

The song opens with a lilting harp gesture played in a minor mode on the reconstructed golden lyre. Over this simple riff, Conner brings the narrative to life using evocative word painting. The realism of her setting creates a sense of immediacy and urgency as if the horrors she sings about happened just yesterday instead of written thousands of years ago. Conner creates a sense of spontaneity and intimacy in her performance through a variety of techniques. At first, her voice pulls the words out sweetly from the center of her vocal range. She sings lyrically with just enough breath to create a sense of lightness, airy timelessness, and distance, giving the illusion that the words just seem to pop into her head.[56] The pitches create light dissonances with the ostinato and do not stray far from the modally ambiguous central tonality of D (sitting between modern D minor and modern D Dorian).[57] See figure 5.

Rhythm very approximate - play freely

Figure 5. Lyre riff.

However, as "the calm of the storm god passed across the sky" (1:50), as the waves crashed, the thunder rumbled, and destruction wiped out humanity, the tessitura changes; Conner digs deep into chesty guttural growls, deftly plays with aspirated consonants, and then swoops up to piercing cries, yelps, and shouts, as depicted in the text. When the gods look down on earth and are unable to recognize the destruction they've caused (2:39), Conner brings her dynamics down to an introspective whisper. When Ishtar screams like a woman in childbirth (3:15–3:35), it is represented in a sustained high a" in the voice. Another mother goddess, Belet-ili, then laments the death of humanity, and Conner represents this goddess's words by descending to a low A:

> Indeed the past has truly turned to clay,
> Because I spoke evil in the assembly of the gods.
> How did I speak evil in the assembly of the gods,
> And declare a war to destroy my people?
> It is I that gave birth to them—my own people! (3:45–4:25)

The song ends with reflective weeping. Conner repeats the final line "The gods, the Anunnaki,[58] were weeping with her [Belet-ili]" on a low intoned A (5:10).

A composer and singer with a PhD in composition, training in early music performance, and an interest in ancient languages,

Conner made an ideal collaborator.[59] After selecting texts from Anne Kilmer's 2012 translation and transliteration of ancient Sumerian and Mesopotamian works,[60] she took inspiration from a wide range of music to write a new setting of the ancient text: she studied sung narratives from China and Portugal as well as Christian Syriac chant, including recordings of Sister Marie Keyrouz. Add to that a healthy sprinkling of Diamanda Galas, Björk, Meredith Monk, and a dash of some metal; all of these sources are audible in *The Flood*.[61]

The music for the album began as improvisations since Lowings does not read standard western music notation.[62] *The Flood* is sung entirely in ancient Mesopotamian languages (Sumerian and Babylonian), but the music is new. The CD liner notes state, "The music is contemporary and original, but imbued with tiny glimmers of a style that may well have sounds in common with the music that was originally sung in Mesopotamia."[63] Those glimmers are in the modes selected for the improvisations based upon the scholarly work of Anne Kilmer, Marcelle Duchesne-Guillemin, Richard L. Crocker, and Martin L. West.

I'm not particularly interested in getting deep into the weeds of ancient Mesopotamian tuning controversies here.[64] Musicologists and Assyriologists carried out the earliest scholarship on ancient Mesopotamian and Sumerian music in the 1960s and 1970s with the discovery of new cuneiform sources from the ancient city of Ugarit.[65] Kilmer and Crocker at the University of California, Berkeley, carried out a series of projects deciphering the collection of hymns and performing them. Their 1976 recording *Sounds from Silence: Recent Discoveries in Ancient Near Eastern Music* included a detailed booklet outlining the researchers' methods, discussions of tuning, instrument reconstruction, and music theory.[66] Kilmer and Crocker argued that the scales used by the ancient Mesopotamians and Sumerians very closely resembled tuning practices described by the Ancient Greeks thousands of years later. More recently, John C. Franklin has demonstrated how Ancient Mesopotamian and

Sumerian lyre tuning systems influenced the Greek lyric tradition as well.[67] Since their work in the 1960s and 1970s, other musicologists and Assyriologists have attempted reconstructions of these ancient musical and music theory texts. Needless to say, there are differing opinions on how these instruments may have been tuned and how the Sumerian and Babylonian languages may have been pronounced, resulting in a very wide variety of schools of decipherment and interpretation.[68]

Conner told me how she set parameters for her improvisations that drew from both ancient and modern musical sources and traditions. She restricted herself to the modes described in the cuneiform tablet sources that, as translated by Kilmer and West, are very similar to Greek modes and also traditional pentatonic Eritrean lyre tunings, as suggested by her collaborator Lowings. Conner, paraphrasing Taruskin, stated that it doesn't really matter if that's the way it sounded: "What matters is feeling. What might it have *felt* like to play music then." The goal was to make music that was "emotionally sincere" and to make an "empathetic connection." "We want to relate to the words. We wanted to feel like it meant. We wanted to draw from what we knew that was the extent. . . . I've read my Taruskin."[69]

The CD's liner notes paint things a bit differently, emphasizing the fidelity to Babylonian sources and minimizing the composer's creative influences: "Stef memorized Babylonian and Sumerian poems and internalized their likely stress patterns (following Kilmer and West) in order to improvise melodic lines in the Mesopotamian modes that sounded as organically 'Babylonian' as possible, but which were ultimately created entirely in her own style."[70] The booklet provides a final caveat reminding us that little is known about Sumerian pronunciation, so much of the performance relies on imagination, but there is no mention of Meredith Monk or Diamanda Galas. It does acknowledge that Lowings drew inspiration from world harp traditions. The CD booklet states, "Andy's lyre accompaniment patterns are derived from the mottled pool of influences he accumulated during his travels in Africa and the Middle East, studying lyre-playing traditions that exponents claim are descended from the ancient Near-East."[71] So Conner and Lowings do not claim their music to *be* ancient Mesopotamian.

The press, however, has latched on to the "authenticity" of Conner's work. She has been interviewed in *Newsweek* and *New Scientist*, among other popular magazines. Conner has expressed frustrations to me with these interviews. She claims that reporters and editors have slapped headlines on the pieces that do not properly represent what she is trying to do.[72] For example, the *New Scientist* lead reads, "I'm reverse-engineering Mesopotamian hit songs," which Conner insists she never said. Although the headline may make great clickbait, it is not representative of her philosophy or her work.[73] Regardless of how many times Conner says publicly that this is new music, the editors and authors of the headlines fall into the trap of seeing the performance as part and parcel of the material reconstruction. When material and performance reconstructions are presented together, many audiences default to the material. "Extreme early music" seems to suggest that new music becomes ancient because either the real relics of ancient cultures or their simulacra trick our rational capacities to distinguish between real and fake, past and present, even if we've "read our Taruskin." Without musical scores, or large quantities of other supporting musical documents to perform long-lost works, anyone can perform authentically ancient music so long as they feel it. However, what makes audiences and performers "feel it" is rarely the performance itself, but usually the material things they see.

CONCLUSION: EVERLASTING LIFE

Conner's song ends with the gods weeping over the earth they ruined, but Tablet XI continues: for six days and seven nights the storms raged and then they stopped. Utnapishtim looked upon the world and saw that "the whole human race had turned to clay.

/ The landscape was flat as a rooftop."[74] Regretful of their harsh punishment of humanity, the gods grant everlasting life to Utnap-ishtim and his wife. Gilgamesh ultimately leaves the "Distant One" without everlasting life. Although he takes back a parting gift, a plant of rejuvenation, he is never able to experience this gift him-self, as it is stolen by a snake.[75] In the end, Gilgamesh returns to his home city of Uruk with a story of the great flood. The narrative gains everlasting life but not its bearer.

Gilgamesh is the perfect metaphor for the reconstructed harps and arches and the newly invented music of the ancient Sumeri-ans. Like Gilgamesh himself, the music is merely the storyteller and the historian. And the history this music tells is not solely for other historians but for all people. The public performance of history (real, imagined, or destroyed) inspires many musicians to perform the past; made accessible, it reenacts destruction and rebirth. Gilgamesh believes he never should have set out on his search for everlasting life; he fears he failed in his quest, but this is the moral of the story: as scholars, we often mistake our suc-cesses as failures. Although sharing the tale with the world may not have been the goal, everlasting life—sharing the tale with the *future*—is the real prize. Monuments, museums, and trium-phal arches don't stand forever. War, violence, time, neglect, and human stupidity destroy all. As *The Epic* proclaims, "Nothing at all has lasted." What survives is the process of history. The telling anew of history endures: reconstructed and reperformed again and again.

NOTES

1. Samuel N. Dorf, *Performing Antiquity: Ancient Greek Music and Dance from Paris to Delphi, 1890–1930* (Oxford: Oxford University Press, 2018), https://global.oup.com/academic/product/performing-antiquity-9780 190612092?cc=us&lang=en&.

2. Kareem Shaheen and Ian Black, "Beheaded Syrian Scholar Refused to Lead

Isis to Hidden Palmyra Antiquities," *Guardian*, August 19, 2015, https://www.theguardian.com/world/2015/aug/18/isis-beheads-archaeologist-syria.

3. The United Nations Educational, Scientific and Cultural Organization (UNESCO) designates landmarks or areas around the globe that are "of outstanding universal value" and meet a number of criteria (https://whc.unesco.org/en/criteria/). UNESCO describes the significance of the site at Palmyra as follows: "An oasis in the Syrian desert, north-east of Damascus, Palmyra contains the monumental ruins of a great city that was one of the most important cultural centres of the ancient world" (see UNESCO, "Site of Palmyra," UNESCO World Heritage List, accessed December 26, 2019, https://whc.unesco.org/en/list/23/). From the 1st to the 2nd century, the art and architecture of Palmyra, standing at the crossroads of several civilizations, married Graeco-Roman techniques with local traditions and Persian influences."

4. Kareem Shaheen, "Isis Blows up Arch of Triumph in 2,000-Year-Old City of Palmyra," *Guardian*, October 5, 2015, https://www.theguardian.com/world/2015/oct/05/isis-blows-up-another-monument-in-2000-year-old-city-of-palmyra.

5. Benjamin Isakhan and Jose Antonio Gonzalez Zarandona, "Erasing History: Why Islamic State Is Blowing up Ancient Artefacts," The Conversation, June 4, 2017, https://theconversation.com/erasing-history-why-islamic-state-is-blowing-up-ancient-artefacts-78667.

6. Roger Michel, "Home," The Institute for Digital Archeology, accessed September 12, 2020, http://digitalarchaeology.org.uk/.

7. In the UK, Ireland, Australia, India, Pakistan, and New Zealand, the gesture of raising the index and middle fingers splayed with the back of the hand facing out is a vulgar gesture akin to the American use of the middle finger. Live Satellite News, "Boris Johnson Unveils Palmyra Arch, London (4–19–16)," YouTube, accessed June 14, 2018, https://youtu.be/n6d7pFBEdPk.

8. Stef Conner, "Discography: *The Flood*," Stef Conner, accessed September 12, 2020, http://www.stefconner.com/music/the-flood-2/.

9. See Andy Lowings, "Introduction & Background," Lyre of Ur Project, accessed December 23, 2019, http://www.lyre-of-ur.com/intro.htm.

10. BBC News, "How Did the Elgin Marbles Get Here?" Entertainment & Arts, December 5, 2014, https://www.bbc.com/news/entertainment-arts-30342462.

11. Emily Cochrane, "Iraqi Artifacts Once Bought by Hobby Lobby Will Return Home," *New York Times*, May 2, 2018, https://www.nytimes.com/2018/05/02/us/politics/iraq-artifacts-hobby-lobby-ice.html.

12. James Cuno, *Who Owns Antiquity? Museums and the Battle over Our Ancient Heritage* (Princeton, NJ: Princeton University Press, 2008), 9–10.

13. John Henry Merryman, "The Nation and the Object," *International Journal of Cultural Property* 1 (1994): 61–76.

14. Kwame Anthony Appiah offers a contrasting argument in support of a cosmopolitanism where we are citizens of the world and argues that what separates us, what creates "others" and "difference," has been overemphasized. Cosmopolitanism, he claims, is "universality plus difference." See Kwame Anthony Appiah, *Cosmopolitanism: Ethics in a World of Strangers* (New York and London: W. W. Norton, 2006), 151.

15. Edward W. Said, *Culture and Imperialism* (New York: Vintage, 1993), 9.

16. Said, *Culture and Imperialism*, xiii.

17. See Billie Melman, "Ur: Empire, Modernity, and the Visualization of Antiquity Between the Two World Wars," *Representations* 145, no. 1 (Winter 2019): 129–51.

18. The British Museum, *Queen's Lyre*, Southern Iraq, Sumerian, about 2600–2400 BC, from Ur; Lapis lazuli, shell, red limestone and gold (H. 112 cm), Excavated by C. L. Woolley, ANE 121198a, https://www.britishmuseum.org/collection/object/W_1928-1010-1-a.

19. Penn Museum, *Lyre Fragment Plaque*, 2450 BCE, University Museum Expedition to Ur, Iraq, 1928; shell, bitumen (L. 31.5 cm x W. 11 cm. x D. 1.5 cm), U.10556 - Field No SF, https://www.penn.museum/collections/object/4466.

20. For more on the looting of the Iraqi Museum and the subsequent investigation to find the missing and stolen materials, see Michael Bogdanos, "The Causalities of War: The Truth about the Iraq Museum," *American Journal of Archaeology* 109, no. 2 (July 2005): 477–526.

21. Very often this desire to reconstruct a destroyed artifact stems from the feeling that the destruction was a personal attack. This is despite the fact that the reconstructors discussed here were not directly impacted by the wars in Iraq or Syria.

22. All Mesopotamia, "Q&A: Andy Lowings, a Reincarnated Ancient Mesopotamian (I'm Pretty Sure)," All Mesopotamia, November 11, 2011, https://allmesopotamia.wordpress.com/tag/andy-lowings/.

23. Andy Lowings, "Harpist Andy Lowings," Spanglefish, accessed September 12, 2020, http://www.spanglefish.com/harpistandylowings/.

24. Lowings provided a detailed narrative of the evolution of his project in a talk delivered at the Library of Congress in 2009. See Andy Lowings, "Lyre of Ur Project," lecture presented at the Library of Congress, Washington, DC, March 17, 2009, accessed December 18, 2019, https://www.loc.gov/item/webcast-4548.

25. Lowings, "Lyre of Ur Project."

26. Lowings, "Lyre of Ur Project." The city of Ur is also the legendary birthplace of Abraham, the founder of many of the world's monotheistic faiths: Judaism, Christianity, and Islam, among others.

27. Roger Michel, interview by Scott Simon, NPR, Weekend Edition Saturday, April 2, 2016, https://www.npr.org/2016/04/02/472784720/upon-reclaiming-palmyra-the-controversial-side-of-digital-reconstruction.

28. Michel, interview by Simon.

29. Quoted in Simon Jenkins, "After Palmyra, the Message to Isis: What You Destroy, We Will Rebuild," *Guardian*, March 29, 2016, https://www.theguardian.com/commentisfree/2016/mar/29/palmyra-message-isis-islamic-state-jihadis-orgy-destruction-heritage-restored.

30. Tim Williams, "Syria: The Hurt and the Rebuilding," *Conservation and Management of Archaeological Sites* 17, no. 4 (November 2015): 300.

31. Sultan Barakat, "Postwar Reconstruction and the Recovery of Cultural Heritage: Critical Lessons from the Last Fifteen Years," in *Cultural Heritage in Postwar Recovery*, ed. Nicholas Stanley-Price (Rome: ICCROM, 2007), 29.

32. Sultan Barakat, "Post-War Reconstruction and Development: Coming of Age," in *After the Conflict: Reconstruction and Development in the Aftermath of War*, ed. Sultan Barakat (London: I. B. Tauris, 2005), 11.

33. The Institute for Digital Archeology, "City Hall Park, New York City," exhibition announcement, September 19–23, http://digitalarchaeology.org.uk/new-york-city/; The Institute for Digital Archeology, "World Government Summit, Dubai UAE," announcement, February 11–14, 2017, http://digitalarchaeology.org.uk/dubai/; The Institute for Digital Archeology, "G7 della Cultura 2017, Florence, Italy," announcement, March 27–April 27, 2017, http://digitalarchaeology.org.uk/florence/; Dubai Future Foundation, "The Triumphal Arch In Arona," announcement, Khaled al-Asaad Archaeological Museum, Arona Italy, April 29, 2017, https://www.archinitaly.org/; The Institute for Digital Archeology, "The National Mall, Washington, DC, USA," announcement, September 26–28, 2018, http://digitalarchaeology.org.uk/washington-dc/.

34. Robert Layton and Julian Thomas, "Introduction: The Destruction and Conservation of Cultural Property," in *Destruction and Conservation of Cultural Property*, ed. Robert Layton, Peter G. Stone, and Julian Thomas (Abingdon, UK, and New York: Routledge, 2011), 1.

35. Seth Doane, "ISIS Destroyed Monuments Reconstructed," CBS Evening News, October 16, 2016, https://www.cbsnews.com/video/isis-destroyed-monuments-reconstructed/.

36. Stef Conner, "Home," Stef Conner, accessed September 12, 2020, http://www.stefconner.com/.

37. Prior to his collaboration with Conner, Lowings worked with Assyriologist Anne Kilmer and harpist Laura Govier. Kilmer and Govier produced their own creations based upon the Silver Lyre of Ur. See Lorna Govier and Anne Kilmer, *The Silver Lyre: New Music for a Mesopotamian Lyre* (Tucson, AZ: Southwest Harp, 2012).

38. Stef Conner, Skype interview with author, June 12, 2018.

39. See Iain Morley, *The Prehistory of Music: Human Evolution, Archaeology, and the Origins of Musicality* (Oxford and New York: Oxford University Press, 2013).

40. See Peter Kivy, *Authenticities: Philosophical Reflections on Musical Performance* (Ithaca, NY, and London: Cornell University Press, 1995); Nicholas Kenyon, ed., *Authenticity and Early Music* (Oxford: Oxford University Press, 1988); John Butt, *Playing with History: The Historical Approach to Musical Performance* (Cambridge and New York: Cambridge University Press, 2002); and Nick Wilson, *The Art of Re-Enchantment: Making Early Music in the Modern Age* (Oxford and New York: Oxford University Press, 2014). Gary Tomlinson draws upon evolutionary theory, nonlinear histories, and other models from anthropology to write about the musical capabilities of human's earliest ancestors. See Gary Tomlinson, *A Million Years of Music: The Emergence of Human Modernity* (Brooklyn: Zone Books, 2015).

41. Rebecca Schneider, *Performing Remains: Art and War in Times of Theatrical Reenactment* (London and New York: Routledge, 2011), 10.

42. Rebecca Schneider, "Rebecca Schneider: Professor of Theatre Arts and Performance Studies," Brown University, accessed September 12, 2020, https://vivo.brown.edu/display/rcschnei.

43. Schneider, *Performing Remains*, 10.

44. Richard Taruskin, "The Pastness of the Present and the Presence of the Past [1988]," in *Text and Acts: Essays on Music and Performance* (New York and Oxford: Oxford University Press, 1995), 99.

45. Taruskin, "The Pastness of the Present," 148.

46. Taruskin, 98.

47. Taruskin, 147

48. Taruskin, 150.

49. See Benjamin R. Foster, "Introduction" to *The Epic of Gilgamesh: A Norton Critical Edition*, ed. and trans. Benjamin R. Foster (New York and London: W. W. Norton, 2001), xx. Like *The Iliad* and *The Odyssey* in the Homeric tradition, *The Epic of Gilgamesh* was most likely a written tradition recited for members of court, not an oral tradition. See Foster, "Introduction," xiv.

50. Tablet X, *The Epic of Gilgamesh*, 81. I cite a few of my favorite English

translations of the Gilgamesh tale in this essay to offer readers a taste of the diversity of approaches.

51. Tablet X, David Ferry, *Gilgamesh: A New Rendering in English Verse* (New York: Farrar, Straus & Giroux, 1992), 64.

52. Tablet XI, *The Epic of Gilgamesh*, 84.

53. Tablet XI, 85.

54. Vanessa Agnew, "Introduction: What Is Reenactment?" *Criticism* 46, no. 3 (Summer 2004): 330.

55. Tablet XI, *The Epic of Gilgamesh*, 87.

56. Mark Harmer, "Stef Conner / The Lyre Ensemble / Union Chapel 2016," Vimeo, June 26, 2017, https://vimeo.com/223171700.

57. Without a leading tone or sixth-scale degree, the ostinato cannot establish D minor nor modern D Dorian.

58. Wikipedia, "Anunnaki," Wikipedia, accessed September 12, 2020, https://en.wikipedia.org/wiki/Anunnaki.

59. Conner's PhD is from the University of York (UK). She studied voice with Anna Maria Friman of Trio Mediaeval and John Potter of the Hilliard Ensemble.

60. Govier and Kilmer, *The Silver Lyre.*

61. Stef Conner, Skype interview with author, June 12, 2018.

62. Subsequently, Conner has written out some of the instrumental parts so that she can perform the songs with other musicians. Stef Conner, email message to author, April 27, 2018; and Stef Conner, Skype interview with author, July 10, 2018.

63. The Lyre Ensemble, *The Flood*, The Lyre of Ur, 2014, CD booklet, 3.

64. The majority of scholars affirm that the surviving documents describe a seven-note diatonic scale achieved through a tuning process of ascending fifths and descending fourths. Describing the Hurrian Hymn in his *Oxford History of Western Music*, Richard Taruskin described the music as "remarkably similar to what we've got now." Richard Taruskin, *Oxford History of Western Music*, 6 vols. (Oxford: Oxford University Press, 2005), 1: 31–32. Also see Anne Draffkorn Kilmer, Richard L. Crocker, and Robert R. Brown, *Sounds from Silence: Recent Discoveries in Ancient Near Eastern Music* (Berkeley, CA: Bit Enki, 1976), 8–11.

65. Marcelle Duchesne-Guillemin, "Découverte d'une gamme babylonienne," *Revue de Musicologie* 49 (1963): 3–17; Anne D. Kilmer, "The Discovery of an Ancient Mesopotamian Theory of Music," *Proceedings of the American Philosophical Society* 115, no. 2 (April 1971): 131–49; Anne D. Kilmer, "The Cult Song with Music from Ancient Ugarit: Another Interpretation," *Revue d'Assyriologie*

et d'archéologie orientale 68, no. 1 (1974): 69–82; Oliver R. Gurney, "An Old Babylonian Treatise of the Tuning of the Harp," *Iraq* 30, no. 2 (Autumn 1968): 229–235; Richard L. Crocker, "Remarks on the Tuning Text UET VII 74 (U. 7/80)," *Orientalia* 47, no. 1 (1978): 99–104; and Hans G. Güterbock, "Musical Notation in Ugarit," *Revue d'Assyriologie et d'archéologie orientale* 64, no. 1 (1970): 45–52.

66. Kilmer, Crocker, and Brown, *Sounds from Silence*, 8–11.

67. John C. Franklin, "Epicentric Tonality and the Greek Lyric Tradition," in *Music, Text, and Culture in Ancient Greece*, ed. Tom Phillips and Armand D'Angour (Oxford and New York: Oxford University Press, 2018), 17–46.

68. I was never formally trained as a scholar of ancient history, archaeology, or linguistics; I am a musicologist and try to understand the ways twentieth and twenty-first century musicians, dancers, and scholars imagine(d) and perform(ed) ancient music and dance. I have read the scholarship on ancient music not just to understand it and compare it to the work of modern performers, but also because the performers of extreme early music have read it as well and often refer to the scholarship of Martin L. West and Stefan Hagel, among others. See Martin L. West, *Ancient Greek Music* (Oxford: Clarendon Press, 1992); Stefan Hagel, *Ancient Greek Music: A New Technical History* (Cambridge: Cambridge University Press, 2009); Richard Crocker, "Mesopotamian Tonal Systems," *Iraq* 59 (1997): 189–202; Anne D. Kilmer, "Musik A. I. in Mesopotamien," in *Reallexikon der Assyriologie und vorderasiatischen Archäologie*, ed. Erich Ebeling and Bruno Meissner (Berlin: De Gruyter, 1997): viii, 463–82; Oliver R. Gurney and Martin L. West, "Mesopotamian Tonal Systems: A Reply," *Iraq* 60 (1998): 223–27; Martin L. West, "The Babylonian Musical Notation and the Hurrian Melodic Texts," *Music and Letters* 75 (1993/1994): 161–179; Theo J. H. Krispijn, "Beitrage zur alrorientalischen Musikforschung 1. Šulgi und die Musik,"*Akkadica* 70 (November/December 1990): 1–27; Sam Mirelman, "A New Fragment of Music Theory from Ancient Iraq," *Archiv für Musikwissenschaft* 67 no. 1 (2010): 45–51; Sam Mirelman and Theo J. H. Krispijn, "The Old Babylonian Tuning Text UET VI/3 899," *Iraq* 71 (2009): 43–52; Anne D. Kilmer and Jeremie Peterson, "More Old Babylonian Music-Instruction Fragments from Nippur," *Journal of Cuneiform Studies* 61 (2009): 93–96.

69. Conner, Skype interview with author, July 10, 2018.

70. *The Flood*, CD booklet, 3

71. *The Flood*, 3.

72. Conner, Skype interview with author, June 12, 2018; Conner, Skype interview with author, July 10, 2018; and Stef Conner, personal conversation with author, December 12, 2018.

73. Stef Conner, interview by Mick Hamer, "I'm Reverse-Engineering Mesopotamian Hit Songs," *New Scientist*, September 17, 2014, https://www.newscientist.com/article/2009121-im-reverse-engineering-mesopotamian-hit-songs/.

74. Tablet XI, *The Epic of Gilgamesh*, 88.

75. Gilgamesh abandons the rejuvenating plant for a moment only to see a snake devour it. Weeping, he cries, "What shall I do? The journey has gone for nothing. / For whom has my heart's blood been spent? For whom? /For the serpent who has taken away the plant. / I descended into the waters to find the plant /and what I found was a sign telling me to abandon the journey and what it was I sought for." Tablet XI, *Gilgamesh*, 81.

AN INTERMEDIA APPROACH TO SEVENTEENTH-CENTURY ENGLISH POPULAR SONG CULTURE

Sarah F. Williams

My scholarly work, and indeed most of my musical interests, always seems to have been concerned with the margins. As a petulant teenager, I had a healthy disdain for popular music that was even remotely considered mainstream. As a liberal arts college student, I was intent on creating as many independent study courses as possible in an effort to supplement my curriculum. When I came to graduate school, I was more intrigued by evidentiary gaps rather than the established historical record. Inspired by a seminar on music and magic in the early modern world taught by Linda Austern at Northwestern University, my dissertation examined how sixteenth- and seventeenth-century English witchcraft was represented in popular entertainments, including street balladry and theater. My first book project, expanded from the broadside ballad chapter of my dissertation, explored the acoustic representations of witchcraft and transgressive women in English broadside ballads. Thus, much of my work deals with descriptions of sound, traces of musical notation, and cultural attitudes toward popular song and music.

With undergraduate degrees in both music and literary studies, I have always felt in between *in terms of disciplinary methodologies. While I collect and draw conclusions from evidentiary support, I marry this historical approach with techniques drawn from literary theory, gender studies, performance studies, and the memory arts to fill in the gaps. One of my earliest influences for an* in between *methodology was a book by Bruce Smith called* The Acoustic World of Early Modern England: Attending to the O-Factor.[1] *Smith's work is essential reading for historical musicologists and literary scholars interested in everything from acoustemology[2] and soundscapes, to music in William Shakespeare's theaters. Smith examines rhetorical manuals, theater schematics, architectural plans, musical examples, and descriptions of ambient sounds; he combines this documentary evidence with a phenomenological approach—that is, a methodology that focuses less on text and objects and more on the experience of, in this case, sound. Smith asks important questions about how listening and acoustic events shape a particular person, group, or cultural identity.*

Smith's work has profoundly shaped my own research for traditional print venues like journals and essay collections. I continue to explore methodologies that can bridge the gap between the textual traces of music and sound and what it was like to actually experience acoustic and performative events in the seventeenth century. Most recently, I've become interested in using the early modern-memory arts as a lens through which to understand cross-references and associations in broadside ballads, theater, and popular song. My newest project, however, is a large-scale digital humanities project called Early Modern Songscapes.[3] *This open-access site offers users a chance to see, hear, and explore early modern English ayres, or songs with a primary vocal line. The first phase features a digital edition of Henry Lawes's 1653 songbook* Ayres and Dialogues.[4] *Rather than listing songs in an archival or database format, information for each song is arranged as a "songscape," which makes available a nonhierarchical, cloud-like array of performative and textual variants and alternate versions of a given song. Much like this essay, with its hyperlinks to audiovisual examples and digital tools, Early Modern Songscapes has shown me the possibilities for web-based visualization of the complex and dynamic interrelationships between song, text, and genre in seventeenth-century England. I hope projects like these will continue to bring together scholars, practitioners, educators, and dramaturgs who hope to reimagine and reanimate the preservation and performance of early modern English music.*

I was to sing them a Song for my money; so I sung them an old Song, the burden of the Song, *Oh women, women, monstrous women, what do you mean for to do?* but because the Song was against women, they would have had me given them their money back again . . . so then I sung them *Doctor* Faustus *that gave his Soul away to the Devill*; for I knew Conjurers and Devills pleased women best.[5]

Some readers might skip over this section in Margaret Cavendish's 1668 closet drama *The Comical Hash* because it contains some antiquated musical references that might not seem immediately relevant to the plot of this seventeenth-century English satire. Students of music history can, and should, find great interest in the richness of this short exchange. While we may not be able to immediately delight in the satirical humor of this scene, with some research, we can begin to reconstruct the complex networks of cross-reference and "intermedia" circulation that makes this dramatic moment resonate for a seventeenth-century listener.[6] Instead of considering works in isolation—just a play, or just a reference to a song or musical composition—we can examine the points of connection within music, text, and performance, and their presentations and *transformations* across different media. Song in particular moved between media in the seventeenth century—including composed music, theatrical performance, printed miscellanies of lyric poetry, commercial publishing, and amateur entertainments. Creating a methodology that acknowledges this movement can only deepen our understanding of the role music played in early modern English culture.

We see examples of intermedial transformation and presentation in our own culture. We recognize bits of classical music sampled in R&B music.[7] We hear a cappella choral arrangements of the latest chart-topping pop song at concerts on college campuses. If we think of the various forms music takes in our culture—for example, academic compositions, pedagogical works, tunes learned through oral transmission over generations, or commercial popular music disseminated in recorded formats—and how these media interact with one another, we might envision a different way of preserving performance or studying historical context. For example, when a commercial music publisher transcribes a notable Broadway or film musical performance that draws upon genres, or types of music, not traditionally associated with Western notation, we might ask the following questions: As music and musical performance moves across media, what is retained from the original performance? What is lost? When the Broadway number is performed at home, is this also a type of theatrical experience? Are there methodologies we can employ or invent to discover the same types of intermedial connections in musical cultures from the seventeenth century?

The following essay sets forth examples for multidisciplinary approaches to seventeenth-century English popular song and its presentations across media by tracing the contextual histories of the tunes mentioned in Cavendish's play as well as a case study involving a popular song arranged by Henry Purcell for Queen Mary. Western culture privileges certain types of media, and historical musicology and literary studies have in turn created hierarchies out of that privilege. A glance at the table of contents for the *Norton Anthology of Western Music* or the *Norton Anthology of English Literature* reveals the priorities of our culture over time—that is, published, notated works written by composers or authors supported by powerful institutions like the Church, aristocratic patrons, or the crown. Yet, to truly understand English musical culture means engaging with not only canonical behemoths like the dramatic works of Shakespeare and his contemporaries, the poetry of John Milton, the Italian operas of G. F. Handel, John Dowland's lute music, the English virginal school,[8] and ballad opera, but also how these works draw on popular songs circulating in London's theaters, streets, and homes. These songs are preserved for us through the notated instrumental compositions of musicians privileged by academic anthologies: Dowland, William Byrd, Orlando Gibbons, and Henry Purcell. Seventeenth-century English popular music and its transmission, reception, and preservation defy the notion of discrete categories of elite and popular, oral and written, high and low, public and private. Our methodologies for studying it should acknowledge this circulation and transformation. Popular song can redefine what performance can be, what a performative space can be. It can reveal a society's priorities, politics, gender and class dynamics, economic trends, tastes, and cultural anxieties.

HOW SEVENTEENTH-CENTURY AUDIENCES KNEW POPULAR MUSIC

In the absence of time travel, we must examine the archival remains, or primary sources, of popular song culture in order to delve deeper into the Cavendish quote above. While recording technology did not exist in the seventeenth century, writings about popular music, instrumental variations on popular tunes, and published ballads offer us some clues. Cavendish's Lady Censurer remarks that she has been asked by the ladies at court to sing "an old Song out of a new Ballad."[9] Her audience has asked her to sing them a well-known song, not anything that would have been notated or composed, but rather a tune immediately recognizable to everyone in the room, regardless of class or generation. These "songs," as the Lady Censurer calls them, were orally circulating melodies during the sixteenth and seventeenth centuries in England used extensively by the broadside ballad trade.[10]

The ultimate intermedia cultural artifact, a broadside ballad, combined music, poetry, visual imagery, and performance.[11] Derived from the medieval dance form, a ballad, or narrative verse set to music, had its roots in dance music (ballade, ballet). The *broadside* ballad was a single-sheet, folio-sized publication printed on one *side*, containing verse, a tune indication, and woodcut imagery that related cautionary tales, current events, and simplified myth and history to a wide range of social classes across early modern England from the 1550s to around 1700. (See figure 1). Broadsides had a very recognizable format and visual appearance, one that remained standard for over a century.[12] They were sold, displayed, and sung in theaters, homes, streets, bookshops, marketplaces, fairs, and taverns—all manner of spaces public, private, and in between.[13] They spread gossip, perpetuated scandals, and regaled audiences with tales of "treasons, murthers, witchcrafts, fires, [and] flouds."[14] Ballads straddled oral and literate culture, the material and the ephemeral, and print and performance. Because of this mutability, the broadside ballad problematizes our notions of a historical text or a musical work in unique ways. Singing, hearing, and seeing ballads was a shared daily experience for most English citizens, an experience that allowed for the constant interaction and metamorphosis of ballad tunes, texts, subject material, and implied social commentary. New ballads referenced old ones, and tunes were recycled for broadsides containing similar subject material.[15] For instance, a particularly popular refrain, or burden, of a broadside ballad might be later printed as a tune title to further capitalize on the success and memorability of the commercially successful sheet. It takes a bit of detective work, but passing references, like the one in Cavendish's play, transmit four-hundred-year-old clues about English popular songs and their cultural meanings.

Figure 1. Thomas D'Urfey, *The Northern Ditty* (London: P. Brooksby, J. Deacon, J. Blare, J. Back, [1685–1688]), EBBA 31817 (http://ebba.english.ucsb.edu/ballad/31817/image).

Let us unpack the humor in Cavendish's scene using the archival remains of broadside ballads. The Lady Censurer's performance begins with a burden, but she decides against it because of its negative connotations. Though she never names the song, a search through the English Broadside Ballad Archive (EBBA)[16] reveals that this burden, "O women, women monstrous women," appears in broadsides, with the late sixteenth-century tune indication "Bragandary." After a while, "Bragandary" disappears as a tune indication from broadside ballads; the tune "Monstrous Women," however, appears later, with poetic verses that match the structure of ballads set to "Bragandary" decades earlier.[17] Ballads set to the "Bragandary" melody, whatever it happened to be titled on the broadside, usually recalled stories of female malfeasance. Since her audience is composed of women, the Lady Censurer ultimately decides upon a different tune to perform. So instead, she settles on a song called "Doctor Faustus." Like "Bragandary," this tune also underwent title transformations. The popular tune "Fortune My Foe" was used at the end of the sixteenth century to accompany a broadside about the ill-fated magician Doctor Faustus.[18] Later, in the seventeenth century, ballads employing the same poetic meter and stanza length appear, calling for their verses to be sung "to the tune of Doctor Faustus." Most of these later texts in some way recall the original subject material of the Doctor Faustus ballad— that is, witchcraft; the supernatural; the last testaments of criminals, warnings, and grisly murder narratives. The Lady Censurer makes reference to these familiar subjects when she remarks that her audience will prefer a tune associated with "Conjurers and Devills."

The tune metamorphoses of "Fortune My Foe" and "Bragandary" were supported through not only the public circulation of broadside-ballad trade but also its rival commercial enterprise: the theaters. The turn of the seventeenth century in England was also the heyday of Shakespeare's plays, productions that were laden with music. The tunes written into and referenced in dramatic works throughout the seventeenth century were popular songs, well-known to the disparate social classes that frequented London's playhouses. Some of the songs were composed for the productions, but most were references to preexisting tunes that were woven into the cultural fabric of the day. Popular songs freely migrated between these media, and playwrights and ballad-writers capitalized on their shared audiences with frequent borrowings and cross-references. Shakespeare's Cleopatra, for instance, hints at the social standing of the ballad-seller when she expresses her contempt for "scald Rimers" who will "Ballad us out a Tune."[19] Likewise, Ophelia famously spouts "Walsingham"[20] and other bawdry as she slips into madness.[21] John Pikering's 1567 play *An enterlude of vice conteyninge, the historye of Horestes* contains the instruction for a song to be sung "to ye tune of have over ye water to floride or selengers round."[22] The tune "Sellenger's Round"[23] was still in wide circulation into the later seventeenth century. A stage direction in George Peele's *Edward the First* indicates "[Enter the Harper, and sing to the tune of Who list to lead a Souldier's life]."[24] Cavendish's play is only one example of a theatrical reference to the tune "Doctor Faustus" or "Fortune my Foe." In Richard Brome's *Antipodes*, the character Joylesse "Whistles Fortune my foe."[25] Thomas Dekker and Samuel Rowley's play features a terrified poet who refuses to write a libel against the king: "[S]hoo'd I be bitter 'gainst the King, / I shall have scurvy ballads made of me, / Sung to the hanging tune."[26] Because of its ghastly associations in the ballad trade, "Fortune my Foe"[27] was often referred to simply as "the hanging tune" in theatrical productions.[28]

Early modern playgoing audiences, from groundlings on the floor to nobility seated in the lord's rooms, experienced multiple layers of meaning as tunes transformed across media: from street song and the ballad trade, through texts recorded in popular miscellanies, to theatrical performance and back again to the streets. This circulation through media ensured a constant metamorphosis of ballad titles and cross-references. For instance, the burden, or refrain, from a popular murder ballad became the new title for the same tune used on a broadside about witches. The same melody whistled on stage in Ben Jonson's latest drama could be heard crudely sung by an itinerant seller competing for sales in London's crowded fairs; plays like Shakespeare's *Titus Andronicus* and *King Lear* would in turn be retold as street ballads.[29] Imagine the business acumen of a broadside ballad-seller, stationed outside a public amphitheater, singing a ballad version of the play being acted within!

HOW WE KNOW SEVENTEENTH-CENTURY POPULAR MUSIC

How did these tunes, in the air and part of the fabric of seventeenth-century culture, come to us in a notated form? How can we reconstruct the sonic experience of a listener upon hearing a theater tune in the streets accompanying a ballad about politics? This is where we see the porous borders between written and oral traditions in the seventeenth century as well as vivid exemplars of seventeenth-century "intermediation," or the interplay and overlap of texts and music across media.

Popular songs were transformed through yet another type of media in the seventeenth century: published song and instrumental collections by what we would consider "canonical" English composers such as William Byrd, Orlando Gibbons, John Dowland, and John Bull, as well as keyboard anthologies like *The Fitzwilliam Virginal Book* and the many editions of John Playford's *The dancing-master*.[30] The pieces in these works were most often in the theme and variation form, as was popular in the sixteenth and seventeenth centuries for collections published for domestic consumption.[31] When translated to the realm of instrumental performance, we get a kind of filtered view of these tunes. Written with the idiomatic capabilities of the instrument for which they are intended, the tunes become highly ornamented, with figurations typical of lute and virginal music of the early seventeenth century. The transmission of these tunes to us through these published works becomes even more complicated when these idiomatic figurations are repeated in popular tune collectors' editions over the centuries. Nineteenth-century compilers like William Chappell and even twentieth- and twenty-first-century scholars like Claude Simpson and Ross Duffin[32] rely upon these instrumental works for notated examples of tunes referenced on seventeenth-century English ballad sheets and in the commercial theater.[33]

We can also glean a more nuanced understanding of the social status of and cultural attitudes toward popular tunes from learned treatises and writings about music. In some cases, we even gain some insight into popular song form and tune titles when notation is not extant. Though these tunes were preserved in published instrumental works by Gentlemen of the Chapel

Royal and learned amateurs, popular song genres, if not specific tunes themselves, received heavy criticism in theoretical treatises such as those by publisher-composer Thomas Morley and critic, poet, and translator William Webbe.[34] Though their commentaries are at times (unintentionally) comically vitriolic, they can offer modern scholars a view into how popular song forms functioned within the zeitgeist of the seventeenth century. Morley hesitates to define popular song as music at all; he reluctantly describes "vinate or drinking songs" as "the slightest kind of music (if they even deserve the name of music)." [35] Enacting a kind of Shakespearean "the lady doth protest too much, methinks" moment, Webbe describes with great specificity the form and composition of the type of popular song that would have accompanied the performance of street balladry:

> If I let passe the uncountable rabble of ryming Ballet makers, and compylers of senceless sonets who be most busy, to stuffe every stall full of gross devises and unlearned Pamphlets: I trust I shall with the best sort be held excused. For though many such can frame an Alehouse song of five or six score verses, hobbling uppon some tune of a Northern Jygge, or Robyn hodde, or La lubber etc., and perhapps observe the just number of sillables, eyght in one line, sixe in an other, and there withall an A to make a jerke at the end.[36]

Webbe seems to have intimate knowledge of these "senceless sonets." We learn from his description that drinking songs were often five or six verses long with alternating eight- and six-syllable lines of poetry, or what is known as common ballad meter. Webbe also tells us where to find broadsides ("stuffed" in "stalls" or booths in London's publishing district and fairs), where one might hear these tunes (an "alehouse"), and even lists examples of tune titles we can trace, through instrumental variations like those published by Byrd, Gibbons, and Bull. Descriptions like Morley's and Webbe's, though critical of this "common" art form, give modern scholars specific details as to the construction of popular song forms when we lack extant copies or concrete evidence. More importantly, they reveal for us how popular song moved through seventeenth-century English society, occupying a kind of in-between space not easily categorized as popular or elite, high or low, performed or published.

There are, of course, advantages and disadvantages to adhering too closely to notated instrumental music and learned literary descriptions for our understanding of seventeenth-century popular song culture. The advantage is that we have what seems like a concrete example of what the tune "actually sounded like," preserved, in perpetuity, in a kind of abstract code we can understand. What this static notation does not communicate is the *flexibility* of song, its genres and meanings for contemporaneous listeners. It doesn't demonstrate that tunes were raw materials, mined by broadside ballad or theater composers, and customized to fit slightly varying poetic structures or dramatic situations. Learned descriptions might be more nuanced if twenty-first-century scholars understand the disdainful attitudes and social contexts within which the descriptions were written. An intermedia approach to studying popular song, from any century, on the other hand, involves understanding the interconnectivity of rival commercial enterprises—the ballad trade, the music-publishing business, arts criticism and polemics, political pamphlet trades, the public and private theaters—and how tunes were adapted for and understood by a wide range of audiences from disparate socioeconomic backgrounds and literacies. The final section of this essay will demonstrate one such approach that captures the multivalent nature of song culture in seventeenth-century England.

THE STORY OF A TUNE: "COLD AND RAW"

The prolific late seventeenth-century tune "Cold and Raw"[37] is an excellent example of the kind of intermedial "meandering" an

English popular song could do in the seventeenth century. Like most of its late sixteenth- and seventeenth-century predecessors, "Cold and Raw" as a melody existed under many different names. Registered in 1632 to Edward Blackmore, a broadside titled *The little barly-corne* states that it should be sung to the tune "Stingo."[38] John Playford published this tune in the 1651 edition of his *English Dancing Master* under the title "Stingo, Or the Oyle of Barly," and indeed the tune fits with the poetic meter of the broadside *The little barly-corne* (see figure 2). Playford continues to publish the tune under the name "Stingo" until the 1690 edition of the *English Dancing Master*, when it becomes titled "Cold and Raw," and "Stingo" disappears from the table of contents[39] (see figure 3). This new tune title probably resulted from the popularity of a lyric published in the 1688 collection *Comes amoris, II* (see figure 4). Thomas D'Urfey, the famous late-seventeenth-century wit and poet, contributed "A New Scotch Song" to the collection, and it contains the first line "Cold and raw the North did blow."[40] A broadside ballad published around the same time titled *The Northern Ditty, Or the Scotch-Man Out-witted by the Country Damsel*, also contains D'Urfey's text, with the tune indication, "To an excellent New Scotch tune, of Cold and Raw the North did blow, etc. / A Song much in Request at Court." This last part might have been a marketing strategy to suggest the fashionable nature of the melody in order sell more broadside copies; the tune is of course much older.[41] The tune then appears by name on countless other broadsides during the last two decades of the seventeenth century.[42] D'Urfey also publishes the text in his 1690 collection *New poems, consisting of satyrs, elegies, and odes together with a choice collection of the newest court songs set to musick by the best masters of the age*. The verbose title suggests the "elite" nature of the pieces contained within, or perhaps the audience to whom D'Urfey hoped to appeal.[43]

"Cold and Raw" continues its intermedia journey with an anecdote retold by eighteenth-century music historian John Hawkins.[44] Hawkins recounts how English clergyman and bass singer John

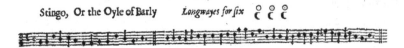

Figure 2. John Playford, *English Dancing Master* (London: John Playford, 1651), 10.

Figure 3. John Playford, *English Dancing Master* (London: John Playford, 1690), 146.

Gostling was invited, along with royal court singer and lutenist Arabella Hunt and famed theater and court composer Henry Purcell, to sing for Queen Mary. After hearing Purcell's music sung before her, the queen allegedly requested Hunt perform the ballad "Cold and Raw." Irritated by this snub, Purcell later incorporated the melody as a ground bass in the verse and ritornello movement "May Her Blest Example"[45] from his birthday ode *Love's Goddess Sure*, Z. 331, to Queen Mary in 1692.[46] (See figure 5.)

From Queen Mary's private chambers, "Cold and Raw" later found its way into London's commercial theaters with some of the most popular works of the early eighteenth century. Developed as a competitor of sorts with imported Italian opera, ballad opera combined popular songs with spoken dialogue. Audiences delighted in the familiarity of ballad opera, both in content and language, as opposed to the *opera seria*, or serious Italian opera, of Handel and others in the first decade of the eighteenth century. "Cold and Raw" appears as a number[47] in one of the most successful ballad operas from this time, John Gay's *The Beggar's Opera* of 1728. The tune appears in a staggering twelve other ballad operas, including Henry Fielding's *Don Quixote in England* (1734). This "Northern

The laſt New Scotch Song.

Ould and Raw the North did blow, Bleak in the Morning Early,

all the Trees were hid with Snow dagled in Winters yearly. As I come riding

on the Slow I met with a Farmers Daughter, with Roſie Cheeks and a

bonny Brow, good Faith made me Mouth to water.

Down I veld my Bonnet low,
  Thinking to ſhow my Breeding,
She return'd a graceful bow,
  A Village far exceeding,
I ask'd her where ſhe went ſo ſoon,
  I long'd to begin a parley ;
She told me to the next Market Town
  On purpoſe to ſell her Barley

In this Purſe ſweet Soul ſaid I
  Twenty pounds lye fairly,
Seek no further one to buy,
  For I'le take all thy Barley,
Twenty more ſhall purchaſe delight,
  Thy Perſon I love ſo dearly,
If thou wot lig with me this Night
  And go home in the Morning early.

If Forty Pounds would buy the Globe,
  This thing I wou'd not do Sir,
Or were my Friends as poor as Job
  I would not raiſe them ſo Sir,
For if this Night you prove my Friend,
  We's get a young Kid together,
And you'l be gon at the Nine Months end,
  And where ſhall I find a Father.

I told her I had Wedded been
  Fourteen Years or longer,
Elſe I would take her for my Queen
  And tye the knot much Stronger,
She bid me then no further come
  But manage my Wedlock fairly,
And keep Purſe for poor Spouſe at home,
  For ſome other ſhould have her Barley.

Figure 4. *Comes Amoris, II* (London: Tho[mas] Moore, 1688), 16.

Figure 5. Henry Purcell, *Love's Goddess Sure Was Blind* (1692), in *The Works of Henry Purcell*, vol. 24, The Purcell Society (London, 1878–1965; 2/1961–), Z. 331. "Cold and Raw" is quoted in a bass line for "May her Blest Example," mm. 343–358.

Ditty" wound its way through London's streets and theater district, published miscellanies, and even court performances, illustrating the fact that popular song was truly without boundaries in the seventeenth century.

CONCLUSION

Popular song in seventeenth-century England was suggested in print on broadside ballads, performed in public and private spaces, referenced and sung on the stage, and notated in the compositions of court and Chapel Royal musicians. Its influence certainly extended to various forms of media available to a wide range of social classes. As a song moves across and through different media, it impresses upon the listener the uniqueness of the new setting but also the familiarity of the known tune. An intermedia approach might also mean studying popular song culture of the seventeenth century through performance. Instead of reading broadside ballads, one could perform them to the indicated tune to determine how well the melody fits the text and if any modifications are necessary. Instead of skipping over song texts in the works of Shakespeare, a useful approach might be to collaborate with dramaturgs or actors to see what possibilities of performance would resonate with audiences today. Perhaps digital approaches to documenting the complex web of cross-reference and musical borrowing would be a more effective way to visualize the intermedia nature of popular song culture as opposed to prose descriptions in traditional print venues. Intermedia approaches reanimate popular song's most ephemeral yet essential facets: its multidimensionality comprised of music, text, and embodied performance; its constant mutability and ability to circulate beyond traditional generic categories; its tendency to create multiple meanings; and its capacity to create new definitions of performative spaces and bodies.

If we engage with an intermedia approach to examine the relevance and resonance of popular song for seventeenth-century audiences, the unbounded possibilities become clear. Song is transformed across media, and these disparate platforms—theatrical experience, "private" court performance, published poetry and instrumental works, broadside ballad circulation, and embodied street performance—leave their own indelible marks on the tune and its reception by the listener. The rich history of song networks and circulation informs how we understand a historical culture's fears, anxieties, politics, and even sense of humor. Ultimately, we can use these approaches to reveal how popular song in our own time moves through and across media to act as powerful social commentary and even, perhaps, an agent of change.

NOTES

1. Bruce Smith, *The Acoustic World of Early Modern England: Attending to the O-Factor* (Chicago: University of Chicago Press, 1999).

2. A worldview centered on sound.

3. University of Toronto at Scarborough, "Early Modern Songscapes: English Ayres and Their Dynamic Acoustic Environments," University of Toronto at Scarborough, accessed September 13, 2020, http://ems.digitalscholarship. utsc.utoronto.ca/.

4. Henry Lawes, *Ayres and Dialogues for 1-3 Voices* (London: T. H. for John Playford, 1653).

5. Margaret Cavendish, *Playes* (London: Printed for John Martyn, James Allestry, and Tho[mas] Dicas, 1662), 573.

6. Examples of critical literature on intermedia studies include Daniel Fischlin, "Introduction," in *OuterSpeares: Shakespeare, Intermedia, and the Limits of Adaptation*, ed. Fischlin (Toronto: University of Toronto Press, 2014), 3–52; and Eric Vos, "The Eternal Network: Mail Art, Intermedia Semiotics, Interarts Studies," in *Interart Poetics: Essays on the Interrelations of the Arts and Media*, ed. Ulla Britta Lagerroth, Hans Lund, and Erik Hedling (Amsterdam: Rodopi, 1997), 325–36.

7. For example, Janet Jackson's "Someone to Call My Lover," *All for You*, Virgin, 2001, includes a representation of Erik Satie's *Gymnopedié No. 1*, first published in *La Musique des Familles (Musique populaire); Journal hebdomadaire illustré* 7, no. 357 (August 1888).

8. Google Scholar, "instrument virginal keyboard OR historical OR early," web search, accessed September 13, 2020, https://en.wikipedia.org/wiki/ English_Virginalist_School.

9. Cavendish, 573.

10. The various uses of broadside ballads—from firestarters and wallpaper to toilet paper—are well documented in seventeenth-century writings. See, for

example, Sir William Cornwallis, "Of the Observation and Use of Things," in *Essayes* (London: Edmund Mattes, 1600), sig. 16-17v, wherein he mentions that he makes use of broadsides in the "privy," employing them as "waste paper." See also Tessa Watt, *Cheap Print and Popular Piety, 1550-1640* (New York: Cambridge University Press, 1991), 192–195. To read and experience early modern English broadside ballads, visit the English Broadside Ballad Archive (EBBA) at http://ebba.english.ucsb.edu for examples and contextual essays. Broadsides cited in this essay contain EBBA catalogue number citations and links when available.

11. Intermedia as a theoretical framework suggests the overlap, interplay, and transformation across media in a much more holistic and integrated way than the term *multimedia*. See Daniel Fischlin, "Introduction," 3–52; and Vos, "The Eternal Network," 325–36.

12. For more information on the standardization of the broadside ballad's visual format, see Tessa Watt, *Cheap Print and Popular Piety* (Cambridge: Cambridge University Press, 1993), 64–79.

13. See George Puttenham, *The Arte of English Poesie* (London: Richard Field, 1598), sig. M1; and William Browne, *Britannia's Pastorals* (London: Geo[rge] Norton, 1613), sig. C2r, for descriptions of various spaces both public and private where broadside ballads were performed.

14. Anonymous, *Witches apprehended, examined and executed, for notable Villanies by them committed both by Land and Water. With a strange and most true Triall how to know whether a Woman be a Witch or not* (London: [William Stansby], 1613), sig. A3v.

15. See Sarah F. Williams, "'A Swearing and Blaspheming Wretch': Representing Witchcraft and Excess in Early Modern English Broadside Balladry and Popular Song," *Journal of Musicological Research* 30, no. 4 (2011): 309–56.

16. English Broadside Ballad Archive, "Home," University of California, Santa Barbara, accessed September 13, 2020, http://ebba.english.ucsb.edu/.

17. See Sarah F. Williams, *Damnable Practises* (Farnham, UK: Ashgate Press, 2015), 74–80, for further commentary on the tune "Bragandary" specifically.

18. *A Ballad of the Life and Deathe of Dr. Faustus, the Great Cungerer* (1589) and *The Judgment of God Shewed upon Dr. John Faustus* (1640?) EBBA 30993, http://ebba.english.ucsb.edu/ballad/30993/image. While the former ballad, a publication that was entered in the Stationers' Register in February 1588–89, no longer survives, it is most likely an earlier edition of the 1640 ballad. Formed in 1403 and chartered in 1557, London's Company of Stationers was a guild of booksellers. All printed works were required to be registered with the company and, according to the charter, any nonregistered or pirated works could

be seized. The company's records provide evidence of publication but not necessarily confirmation that the printed work survives to this day. The register is available and searchable online at https://stationersregister.online/.

19. William Shakespeare, *Antony and Cleopatra*, 5.2.211. All Shakespeare references are from William Shakespeare, *The Oxford Shakespeare: The Complete Works*, 2nd ed. (Oxford: Oxford University Press, 2005).

20. English Broadside Ballad Archive, "EBBA 20102: Magdalene College—Pepys," University of Southern California, Santa Barbara, accessed September 13, 2020, http://ebba.english.ucsb.edu/ballad/20102/recording.

21. William Shakespeare, *Hamlet*, 4.5.24–58. See also Amanda Eubanks Winkler, *O Let Us Howl Some Heavy Note: Music for Witches, the Melancholic, and the Mad on the Seventeenth-Century English Stage* (Bloomington: Indiana University Press, 2006), 86–91, for an in-depth discussion of ballad tunes and Ophelia's madness in Shakespeare's *Hamlet*. See also Leslie Dunn, "Ophelia's Songs in Hamlet: Music, Madness, and the Feminine," in *Embodied Voices: Representing Female Vocality in Western Culture*, ed. Leslie C. Dunn and Nancy A. Jones (Oxford: Oxford University Press, 1994), 50–64.

22. John Pikering, *A newe enterlude of vice conteyninge, the historye of Horestes* (London: Wylliam Gryffith, 1567), sig. Biiv.

23. English Broadside Ballad Archive, "EBBA 33797: National Library of Scotland—Crawford," University of Southern California, Santa Barbara, accessed September 13, 2020, http://ebba.english.ucsb.edu/ballad/33797/recording.

24. George Peele, *The famous chronicle of king Edward the first* (London: William Barley, 1593), sig. C1r.

25. Richard Brome, *The antipodes a comedie* (London: Francis Constable, 1640), sig. G1r. For additional scholarship on song in early modern English theater, see, briefly, Bruce R. Smith, *The Acoustic World of Early Modern England: Attending to the O-Factor* (Chicago: University of Chicago Press, 1999), 206–45; and "Shakespeare's Residuals: The Circulation of Ballads in Cultural Memory," in *Shakespeare and Elizabethan Popular Culture*, ed. Stuart Gillespie and Neil Rhodes (London: Arden Shakespeare, 2006), 193–218; David Lindley, "Song," in *Shakespeare and Music* (London: Arden Shakespeare, 2005), 141–98; Ross Duffin, *Shakespeare's Songbook* (New York: W. W. Norton, 2004), 15–42; and "Ballads in Shakespeare's World," in *"Noyses, sounds and sweet aires": Music in Early Modern England*, ed. Jessie Ann Owens (Washington, DC: Folger Shakespeare Library, 2006), 32–47; Dunn, "Ophelia's Songs in Hamlet," 50–64; Peter Seng, *The Vocal Songs in the Plays of Shakespeare* (Cambridge, MA: Harvard University Press, 1967); Bryan N. S. Gooch and David Thatcher,

A Shakespeare Music Catalogue, 5 vols. (Oxford: Oxford University Press, 1991); Christopher R. Wilson and Michela Calore, *Music in Shakespeare: A Dictionary* (London: Continuum Press, 2008); Stuart Gillespie, "Shakespeare and Popular Song," in *Shakespeare and Elizabethan Popular Culture*, ed. Stuart Gillespie and Neil Rhodes (London: Arden Shakespeare, 2006), 174–92; Linda Phyllis Austern, *Music in English Children's Drama of the Late Renaissance* (Philadelphia, PA: Gordon & Breach, 1992); Howell Chickering, "Hearing Ariel's Songs," *Journal of Musicological Research* 24, no. 1 (1994): 131–72.

26. Samuel Rowley and Thomas Dekker, *The noble souldier* (London: Printed [by John Beale], 1634), sig. D4v.

27. English Broadside Ballad Archive, "EBBA 30084: British Library—Roxburghe," University of Southern California, Santa Barbara, accessed September 13, 2020, http://ebba.english.ucsb.edu/ballad/30084/recording.

28. For recent commentary on "Fortune my Foe," see Christopher Marsh, "'Fortune my Foe': The Circulation of an English Super Tune," in *Intersections. Interdisciplinary Studies in Early Modern Culture: Identity, Intertextuality, and Performance in Early Modern Song Culture*, ed. Dieuwke van der Poel, Wim van Anrooij, and Louis Peter Grijp (Leiden: Brill, 2016), 308–30. For broadsides that use "Fortune my Foe," see the EBBA listings: http://ebba.english.ucsb.edu/.

29. See the ballads *Titus Andronicus Complaint* (London: E. Wright, 1624), EBBA 20040, http://ebba.english.ucsb.edu/ballad/20040/image; *The Tragical History of King Lear* (London: [1700]), EBBA 30989, http://ebba.english.ucsb.edu/ballad/30989/citation, though an earlier version titled *the Tragecall historie of kinge leir and his Three Daughters* is registered to John Wright with the Stationers' Company on May 8, 1605, https://stationersregister.online/entry/SRO4976; *A newe ballad of Romeo and Juliett* was registered with the Stationers' Company to Edward White on August 5, 1596, https://stationersregister.online/entry/SRO3872.

30. John Playford, *The dancing-master* (London: John Playford, 1686). See also Thurston Dart, "New Sources of Virginal Music," *Music and Letters* 35 (1954): 93–106, for descriptions of the most important keyboard manuscripts and printed collections in early modern England. See also Charles Baskervill, *Elizabethan Jig and Related Song Drama* (New York: Dover, 1965), 164–218.

31. For more reading on the problematic nature of the term *domestic music*, see Candace Bailey's "The Challenge of Domesticity in Men's Manuscripts in Restoration England," in *Beyond Boundaries: Rethinking Music Circulation in Early Modern England* (Bloomington: Indiana University Press, 2015), 114–26.

32. Ross W. Duffin, *Some Other Note: The Lost Songs of English Renaissance*

Comedy (Oxford: Oxford University Press, 2018), https://global.oup.com/us/companion.websites/9780190856601/.

33. In addition to Simpson and Duffin, see William Chappell, *The Ballad Literature and Popular Music of the Olden Time* (New York: Dover, 1965).

34. Examples of popular song genres include jigs, rounds, or tavern songs in common meter. See Williams, *Damnable Practises*, 49–88, for more context.

35. Thomas Morley, *A Plaine and Easie Introduction to Practicall Musick* (London: Peter Short, 1597), 295.

36. William Webbe, *A discourse of English poetrie* (London: [J]ohn Charlewood, 1586), sig. D1r. This Shakespeare reference occurs in *Hamlet*, 3.2.218.

37. English Broadside Ballad Archive, "EBBA 31817: University of Glasgow Library—Euing," University of Southern California, Santa Barbara, accessed September 13, 2020, http://ebba.english.ucsb.edu/ballad/31817/recording.

38. *The little barly-corne* (London: E. B[lackmore], [1632]). The *Oxford English Dictionary* defines "stingo" as strong ale or beer, likewise a person full of vim and vigor. "stingo, n,." *Oxford English Dictionary* (Oxford: Oxford University Press, 2018), http://www.oed.com/view/Entry/190404?redirectedFrom=stingo.

39. See also Margaret Dean-Smith and E. J. Nicol, "The Dancing Master: 1651–1728," *Journal of the English Folk Dance and Song Society* 4, no. 3 (1943): 137.

40. *Comes amoris, II* (London: Tho[mas] Moore, 1688), 16; Various Artists, "Cold and Raw," YouTube, January 12, 2015, https://www.youtube.com/watch?v=nMxFQ3Xw_6w.

41. *The Northern Ditty* (London: P. Brooksby, J. Deacon, J. Blare, J. Back, [1685–1688]), EBBA 31817, http://ebba.english.ucsb.edu/ballad/31817/image.

42. For more history on the usage of the tune "Cold and Raw," see Simpson, *The British Broadside Ballad*, 687–692. See also Steve Newman, *Ballad Collection, Lyric, and the Canon: The Call of the Popular from the Restoration to the New Criticism* (Philadelphia: University of Pennsylvania Press, 2007), 19–57.

43. Thomas D'Urfey, *New poems* (London: J. Bullard and A. Roper, 1690), fol. K2v–K3v.

44. John Hawkins, *A General History of Science and Practice of Music,* vol. 3 (London: T. Payne and Son, 1776), 564. See also James Anderson Winn, *Queen Anne, Patroness of the Arts* (Oxford: Oxford University Press, 2014), 157; Roger Fiske, *Scotland in Music: A European Enthusiasm* (Cambridge: Cambridge University Press, 1983), 187.

45. Geoffrey Weber, "May Her Blest Example Chase," YouTube, January 23, 2017, https://www.youtube.com/watch?v=ZtNgUoADVao.

46. Henry Purcell, *Love's Goddess Sure Was Blind* (1692), in *The Works of Henry*

Purcell, vol. 24, The Purcell Society (London, 1878–1965; 2/1961–), Z. 331.

47. RegiioTV, "If Any Wench/A Maid Is Like The Golden Ore (The Beggar's Opera)," YouTube, August 21, 2014, https://www.youtube.com/watch?v=FF5gY-MYVm4.

FURTHER READING

Burke, Peter. *Popular Culture in Early Modern Europe*. New York: Harper & Row, 1978.

_____. "Popular Culture in Seventeenth Century London." In *Popular Culture in Seventeenth-Century England*. Edited by Barry Reay, 31–58. New York: St. Martin's, 1985.

Chappell, William. *The Ballad Literature and Popular Music of the Olden Time*. New York: Dover, 1965.

Duffin, Ross. *Shakespeare's Songbook*. New York: W. W. Norton, 2004.

Fischlin, Daniel. "Introduction." In *OuterSpeares: Shakespeare, Intermedia, and the Limits of Adaptation*. Edited by Daniel Fischlin, 3–52. Toronto: University of Toronto Press, 2014.

Fox, Adam. *Oral and Literate Culture in England, 1500–1700*. Oxford: Oxford University Press, 2000.

Fumerton, Patricia, Anita Guerrini, and Kris McAbee, *Ballads and Broadsides in Britain: 1500-1800*. Farnham: Ashgate Press, 2010.

Marsh, Christopher. *Music and Society in Early Modern England*. Cambridge: Cambridge University Press, 2010.

Monson, Craig. "Songs of Shakespeare's England." In *The World of Baroque Music: New Perspectives*. Edited by George B. Stauffer, 1–24. Bloomington: Indiana University Press, 2006.

Poulton, Diana. "The Black-Letter Broadside Ballad and Its Music," *Early Music* 9 (1981): 427–37.

Reay, Barry, ed. *Popular Culture in Seventeenth-Century England*. New York: St. Martin's, 1985.

Reay, Barry. *Popular Cultures England, 1550–1750*. London: Longman, 1998.

Smith, Bruce R. *The Acoustic World of Early Modern England: Attending to the O-Factor*. Chicago: University of Chicago Press, 1999.

Simpson, Claude. *The British Broadside Ballad and Its Music*. New Brunswick, NJ: Rutgers University Press, 1966.

Vos, Eric. "The Eternal Network: Mail Art, Intermedia Semiotics, Interarts Studies." in *Interart Poetics: Essays on the Interrelations of the Arts and Media*. Edited by Ulla Britta Lagerroth, Hans Lund, Erik Hedling, 325–36. Amsterdam: Rodopi, 1997.

Ward, John. "Apropos the British Broadside Ballad and Its Music." *Journal of the American Musicological Society* 20 (1967): 28–86.

Watt, Tessa. *Cheap Print and Popular Piety, 1550–1640*. Cambridge: Cambridge University Press, 1994.

Williams, Sarah F. "'A Swearing and Blaspheming Wretch': Representing Witchcraft and Excess in Early Modern English Broadside Balladry and Popular Song." *Journal of Musicological Research* 30, no. 4 (2011): 309–56.

_____. "To the Tune of Witchcraft: Witchcraft, Popular Song, and the Seventeenth-Century English Broadside Ballad." *Journal of Seventeenth-Century Music* 19, no. 1 (2013).

_____. *Damnable Practises: Music, Witchcraft, and Dangerous Women in Seventeenth-Century English Broadside Ballads*. Farnham: Ashgate Press, 2015.

_____. "'Lasting-Pasted Monuments': Music, Memory, Theater, and the Early Modern English Broadside Ballad." In *Beyond Boundaries: Rethinking the Circulation of Music in Early Modern England*. Edited by Linda P. Austern, Candace Bailey, and Amanda Eubanks Winkler, 96–113. Bloomington: Indiana University Press, 2017.

Würzbach, Natascha. *The Rise of the English Street Ballad, 1550–1650*. Translated by Gayna Walls. Cambridge: Cambridge University Press, 1990.

INSTRUMENTAL MUSIC IN EARLY SEVENTEENTH-CENTURY ITALY

Instruments as Vehicles of Discovery

Rebecca Cypess

To access all audio/visual examples referenced in this essay, please visit the open access version on Fulcrum at https://doi.org/10.3998/mpub.12063224.

INTRODUCTION

I first encountered the instrumental repertoire of early seventeenth-century Italy as an undergraduate music major, but my earliest immersive experience with it took place when I was a master's student in harpsichord performance. Playing both the solo keyboard music and the chamber music from that revolutionary moment in musical history was transformative for me. I was gripped by the work of composers such as Biagio Marini, Dario Castello, Giovanni Battista Fontana, Carlo Farina, Giovanni Battista Buonamente, Girolamo Frescobaldi, and many others, all of whom were performers as well as composers. I was fascinated by the fluidity of their music, by its elegance, by its balance between careful compositional rigor and wild abandon. Like much other Baroque music, it struck me as rhetorical music—music that captured aspects of patterns of human speech or communication—but also as music that spoke to me on a more basic, emotional level. In fact, as I would come to learn through playing, the Italian instrumental music composed during the first decades of the seventeenth century was simultaneously more *ephemeral* than vocal music, in that it lacks a text to give it precise, specific meanings, and more *material*, in that it addresses the physical properties of the musical instrument itself.

In graduate school and in the years just afterward, I worked on a dissertation that situated this revolutionary instrumental music within the context of the broader Italian musical landscape of the time—especially the dramatic developments in vocal music with which it coincided. Events such as the Artusi–Monteverdi controversy[1] and the invention of the recitative[2] (the basis of opera) have often been regarded as watershed moments in music history, and these have long dominated the discourse around instrumental music too. My dissertation built on this understanding, and, as I have discussed elsewhere,[3] I still think it is true that composers of instrumental music responded to developments in vocal music and vice versa. However, more recently, I have tried to consider how their compositions treat instruments in particular—how they use those instruments, manipulate them, show them off, and sometimes even "misuse" them or handle them in a way that seems "incorrect."

This idiomatic use of instruments was a new phenomenon in musical compositions at the turn of the seventeenth century, and it does not have a clear parallel in vocal music. However, this new interest in the medium of instrumental music may be understood as a manifestation of a fascination with instruments of all sorts—whether musical, artistic, or scientific. As historians of science and visual art have shown, instruments as a broad category—from the sculptor's chisel to the clock and the telescope—had formerly been understood as tools for the repetition of processes already known or the remaking of objects already invented. Around 1600, instruments came to be seen as vehicles of exploration and open-ended inquiry.[4] When Galileo Galilei trained his high-powered telescope on the sky, he did not know what he would see, and he used sensory observation and reason to interpret his observations.[5] Visual artists within Galileo's circle began to incorporate his findings into their depictions of nature and the heavens, thus interpreting what he saw and bringing it to bear on their own creative processes.[6]

The same type of open-ended inquiry, and the same sense of exploration, may be discerned in instrumental music of the early seventeenth century. Musical instruments in the age of Galileo came to be understood as vehicles for discovery, the imitation of nature, and the representation and stimulation of human emotions, or *affetti*. A sense of discovery of the instrument itself is manifested in the new, idiomatic approach that appears in many instrumental compositions of this period. Some works even seem to enact the processes of exploration and discovery, calling attention to staged acts of "improvisation" and to the instrument's physical construction and sonic capabilities.[7]

In what follows, I present three examples that show how some composers of early seventeenth-century Italy came to approach their compositions through their instruments, harnessing their distinctive features in order to evoke ideas, to depict images, and to excavate and explore human emotion. Far from merely imitating the innovations in vocal music, these instrumental composers were pioneers of discovery and invention.[8]

THE BEGINNINGS OF IDIOMATIC INSTRUMENTAL MUSIC IN THE EARLY SEVENTEENTH CENTURY

In order to understand how some instrumental composers in early seventeenth-century Italy broke new ground by inscribing an idiomatic approach within their compositions, it is helpful to understand the foundation on which they were building. In most earlier instrumental music—especially music for ensemble instruments such as consorts of violin-family instruments or wind instruments such as cornettos and trombones—the specific choice of instruments was left open; performers could choose their instrumentation based on what they had available or what they preferred to hear. As a result, the compositions themselves are generally not idiomatic to specific instruments.

The music of the Venetian composer and organist Giovanni Gabrieli (1554/1557–1612) is a case in point. Almost all of Gabrieli's works were published without specific instruments designated. Instead, he labeled each line with a generic name based on its range; for example, *cantus, altus, tenore, bassus,* and so on. In practice, these lines could be executed by string instruments such as those of the violin[9] family (which came, as they still do, in various sizes) or by wind instruments such as cornettos, recorders, trombones, or shawms.[10] As a result, Gabrieli's approach to instrumental composition was flexible. It is likely that he wanted his music to be adaptable to numerous instrument types, both for practical and for artistic reasons. Practically speaking, this would mean that his music could be used by more ensembles in a greater number of churches, even if such institutions lacked access to players of specific instruments. Artistically speaking, Gabrieli and his contemporaries embraced an aesthetic of variety. The sound of a mixed consort, including some wind and some string instruments with varying timbres, perhaps also with organ accompaniment, was attractive.[11] (In some cases, canzonas could be played either on organ or harpsichord alone instead of by a consort of solo-melody instruments.[12])

In this scenario, it was a performer's obligation to render the music in a manner that would be idiomatic to their instrument, making them sound well and exploiting their unique properties. Like most sixteenth-century Italian writers, Gabrieli most likely understood the objective of instrumental music as the imitation of the human voice. Players of each instrument would have to learn how to effect that imitation using the equipment they had—for example, violinists in the management of their bows, and trombonists through a delicate tone (not a blasting one, which was a feature of later music) and meticulous breath control.[13] Silvestro Ganassi, a professional wind player, described this ideal as follows:

> You must know that all musical instruments, in comparison to the human voice, are lacking; therefore we must attempt to learn from it and imitate it. You will object, saying, "How is it possible for this thing to produce words? Because of this [deficiency] I do not believe that this flute could ever be similar to the human voice." And I respond that, just as a worthy and perfect painter imitates everything created in nature through a variety of colors, so with this instrument of wind [or] strings you can imitate the utterances of the human voice.[14]

This recording (see example 1 on Fulcrum) of Gabrieli's "Canzon septimi toni à 8," from his *Sacrae symphoniae* of 1597, uses historical information about performance practices from this period to render the music personalized and idiomatic. The performers, from the Green Mountain Project, improvise embellishments in melodic lines and at the ends of phrases (see audio 1 on Fulcrum). They use a mixed instrumentation of violins and wind instruments. Above all, their phrasing is highly rhetorical and imitates the patterns of human song and speech.

That the vast majority of compositions for instrumental ensemble in the sixteenth century were labeled with the genre-title canzona is suggestive: that genre consisted originally of parodies or imitations of French or Franco-Flemish chansons—that is, vocal music. Even when the canzona became an independent genre in the 1560s–1580s, and composers stopped using preexistent vocal works as the basis of their compositions, they continued to apply vocally based gestures, forms, section types, and melodic motives in their instrumental compositions.

The word "canzona" derives from "cantare," meaning "to sing," and Gabrieli continued to use it when he was writing these pieces for instruments. By the end of the seventeenth century, the canzona had been rendered obsolete, having been supplanted by the *sonata* (from "sonare," to play)—a term that calls attention to the sonic capacities of instruments.[15] While this terminological transition began in Gabrieli's day, it did not occur all at once, and the terms *sonata* and *canzona* were used interchangeably well into the seventeenth century.[16] Nevertheless, the gradual adoption of the term *sonata* to describe a multisection (and later a multimovement) work for instrumental ensemble is telling: it points to a new interest in the idiomatic properties and sounds of musical instruments themselves. Composers began, increasingly, to write for specific instruments rather than any number of interchangeable ones. The sonata exemplified a new type of composition, one that harnessed the physical and sonic properties of those instruments themselves. What could an individual instrument do that was distinct from every other instrument? What unique sounds could it produce? How could it be held, tuned, and played? What habits, what sounds were fostered by the performance techniques that each instrument demanded? In what sense could it serve as a vehicle for exploring human emotions or the natural world?

One composer whose instrumental sonatas pioneered the exploration of these questions was Biagio Marini (1594–1663). Born in Brescia, a city known for its tradition of instrumental performance and lutherie,[17] Marini followed his father and uncle into the profession of music. In 1615, he was appointed violinist at the Basilica of St. Mark, where no less a composer than Claudio Monteverdi was then *maestro di cappella*. A virtuosic violinist, Marini inscribed many of his virtuosic practices into his compositions. He left specific instructions to the performer about the representation of *affetti* (emotions) and about the imitation of the sounds of other instruments on the violin. He also called for the use of extended techniques such as scordatura (literally "mistunings"; i.e., alternative tunings of the violin that deviate from the standard open-fifths tuning) and double- and triple-stops. These representational moments and explorations of the violin as an instrument with unique properties show Marini's interest in the capacities of instruments as vehicles for exploration and discovery.

Marini's first publication, the *Affetti musicali* (1617), consisted of instrumental works, each with a name that indicated a dedication to a particular patron or family of patrons (e.g., "Il Monteverde"). Some of these feature special techniques that call attention to the capacities of instruments that are distinct from voices. For example, "La Foscarina" includes the first known indication of tremolo. This, however, was not the instrumental tremolo of the nineteenth century, but rather a measured bow tremolo in imitation of the "tremulant" of the organ—a mechanism that starts and stops the flow of air through organ pipes at a regular interval of time, resulting in what was understood as a melancholy emotional effect. In "La Foscarina" (see example 2 and audio 2 on Fulcrum) the string instruments are told to use "tremolo con l'arco" (tremolo of the bow) while the basso continuo part, meant to be executed on the organ, says simply "metti il tremolo" (engage the tremulant).

In his impressively titled *Sonate, symphonie, canzoni, pass'emezzi, baletti, corenti, gagliarde, & retornelli* (1626), Marini expanded the list of virtuosic techniques upon which his compositions drew. Published after Marini had left Venice and was employed instead by Duke Wolfgang Wilhelm of Neuberg, Germany, the *Sonate* reflected his patron's tastes for so-called curiosities.[18] Indeed, many members of the nobility in Italy and across Europe had taken to assembling what were known as *Kunstkammern* or *Wunderkammern* (rooms of art and curiosities) to display their interest in art and science. Such collections could include paintings or sculptures, rare animal horns, seashells fused with metal and formed into lavish drinking cups, musical instruments, and countless other wonders. Figure 1 depicts the dedicatee of Marini's *Sonate*, Isabella Clara Eugenia, archduchess of the southern Netherlands, visiting such a Kunstkammer with her husband.[19] It was on the title page of this volume that Marini advertised the "curious and modern inventions"—novel uses of the violin that, taken together, create the same sense of wonder and contemplation that would be elicited by a visit to an early modern Kunstkammer.

Figure 1. Hieronymous Francken the Younger and Jan Brueghel the Elder, *The Archdukes Albert and Isabella Visiting a Collector's Cabinet*, oil on panel, 0.94 m. x 1.233 m., 1621–1623, the Walters Art Museum.

What did Marini's curiosities consist of? In addition to numerous dance pieces that would have served to accompany the social gatherings of his patrons, Marini included instrumental works that feature technical wonders or illusions. For example, his "Sonata quarta per il violino per sonar con due corde" (fourth sonata for the violin to play with two strings; see example 3 on Fulcrum) calls upon the violinist to play passages using double stops—that is, playing on two strings at once. Elsewhere in the same sonata, Marini writes long notes with the rubric *Affetti*, suggesting that the violinist should embellish the melody freely so as to stimulate an emotional response in the listeners. In an important indicator of the aesthetics of the age, Marini seems to be equating ornaments with emotions; improvised ornaments, too, form a sort of curiosity that can stimulate an emotional response. In another case, Marini uses not just double stops but triple stops to allow the violin to imitate another instrument. In the "Capriccio per sonare il violino con tre corde a modo di lira" (capriccio in which the violin plays on three strings in the manner of a *lira*; see example 4 and audio 4 on Fulcrum), the violinist imitates the performance practices of a *lira da braccio*—an instrument prized, especially in the sixteenth century, for its role in accompanying the recitation of poetry.[20]

In one of the most remarkable sonatas of the collection, the *Sonata in ecco* (echo sonata; see example 5 and audio 5 on Fulcrum), scored for three violins, Marini uses not just violinistic feats but also staging to inspire a sense of *meraviglia* (marvel). The sonata opens with a long section for solo violin and continuo, creating the impression that this is another work for a single violin and continuo. However, after this lengthy opening section, the first violinist initiates a section that includes two echoing violins positioned off stage: the second and third parts indicate that "whoever plays this part should not be seen." The sound of the echoing instruments thus emerges mysteriously as disembodied music, forming an example of what Arne Spohr has called "concealed music"—music meant to be heard from chambers adjacent to those in which the patron and his audience were seated.[21] In fact, as modern performances of this piece confirm, the sound of Marini's composed echo merges with the natural echo of the performance space, creating an overwhelming, kaleidoscopic effect. Yet Marini also calls attention to his own dramatic artifice: the first violin plays a passage in double stops, but the echoing instruments divide those double stops between them. Marini thus draws back the curtain, exposing the artifice of his composition.

In some ways, Marini's musical language builds on that of

Gabrieli and his contemporaries. In particular, the sectional organization of Marini's works confirms his indebtedness to the Venetian school of instrumental composition. Like Gabrieli's, Marini's extended instrumental pieces create a sense of interest and variety by moving from one section type to another—changing from duple to triple meter and back again, alternating homophonic and contrapuntal sections, and so on. However, Marini's melodies are less "singable" than Gabrieli's: his language is not rooted in song but in the exploration of his own instrument—the violin. He uses open strings extensively, moves capriciously up and down the fingerboard, and exploits his own virtuosity in order to elicit a sense of wonder and curiosity among his listeners. If his virtuosic flourishes sound like they might be improvised, that is perhaps because they are rooted in the intimate tactile relationship between the player and the instrument. Marini uses the instrument as his starting point, allowing his artisanship and his muscle memory to lead him in new directions.

Marini's contemporaries, as well as later composers of the seventeenth century, likewise turned to the "discovery" of the instrument for compositional inspiration. Carlo Farina's "Capriccio stravagante," published in Dresden, Germany, just a year after Marini's *Sonate*, puts virtuosic violinistic tricks to use in a broader representational project (see example 6 and audio 6 on Fulcrum). He uses *glissando* (sliding the finger up and down the fingerboard) to represent the mewling of cats and barking of dogs, double stops to imitate the folk instrument known as the hurdy-gurdy as well as the dissonant crow of a rooster, *pizzicato* (plucking) to imitate the Spanish guitar, and many others. The *Capriccio*, roughly eighteen minutes in performance, presents an exhaustive tour of a musical Kunstkammer.

The Venetian wind player and composer Dario Castello published two volumes of *Sonate concertate in stil moderno* (concerted sonatas in the modern style, 1621 and 1629).[22] The seventeenth sonata of the second volume—the last in the collection—is an extended work for violin, cornetto, and bass, together with an echo-ing violin and an echoing cornetto (see example 7 and audio 7 on Fulcrum). Here, Castello creates a conspicuous contrast between the idioms of the violin and the cornetto. He writes extended, rhapsodic passages for each of the two main instruments, and they are remarkably different from one another. The violin solo exploits the capability of that instrument, gravitating especially toward open strings and creating figuration that fits easily under the hand of the player. The cornetto solo relies most heavily on passagework in C major and G major, the two keys most idiomatic to that difficult and highly prized instrument.

Some Italian composers continued to write in this virtuosic manner (see, for example, the works of Tarquinio Merula and, especially, Marco Uccellini), but by the end of the seventeenth century, a more conservative, restrained style began to dominate. Most notably, the instrumental publications of Arcangelo Corelli take on a more rhetorical and songlike mode of expression while reducing the physical demands on the performers. (Corelli him-self was a highly virtuosic violinist, but he was apparently pack-aging his published music for an audience of less-accomplished players, including both amateurs and professionals.) However, the last decades of the seventeenth century saw the rise of extreme virtuosity in the violin works of composers in central Europe, such as Heinrich Ignaz Franz Biber (1644–1704), Georg Muffat (1653–1704), and Johann Heinrich Schmelzer (1623–1680).[23] Biber's "Sonata representativa" is similar to Farina's "Capriccio stravagante" in that it uses the violin to imitate sounds of nature. And his famed "Rosary Sonatas," though they were unpublished and little known during Biber's lifetime, stand today as one of the most impressive collections of violin music in the classical corpus. Each of the fifteen sonatas in the collection calls for a different tuning of the violin (using the scordatura practice dis-cussed above), again using music to explore the very nature of the instrument itself.

AN IDIOMATIC APPROACH TO THE HARPSICHORD IN ITALY: GIROLAMO FRESCOBALDI'S *TOCCATE*

The culture of keyboard music in early modern Italy stood apart from that of other instruments. In general, keyboard players were educated in churches, and were thus literate in both music and other fields; they were trained, for example, in music theory as well as Latin and rhetoric. Players of other instruments most often learned their craft through apprenticeship or the oral transmission of information from teacher to student.[24] Partly because of these divergent professional avenues, keyboard repertoire has generally been separately considered from other instrumental music. However, I argue that there are important points of overlap in keyboard practice and the practice of other instruments in the early seventeenth century—especially in the idiomatic approach that I have been discussing. Keyboard composers, too, were influenced by the new conception of instruments that came to the fore in early seventeenth-century Italy.

In the second half of the sixteenth century, as the canzona for instrumental ensembles was on the rise, keyboard canzonas and variations likewise increased in popularity. Composers such as Claudio Merulo (1533–1604) brought this genre to great heights, and his published keyboard canzonas stand out for their complexity, variety, and length. Another genre to which Merulo contributed actively was the toccata. This term, derived from the word *toccare* ("to touch") adds another dimension to the apparent contrast between the canzona and the sonata. The implication of this title is that the composer invents the music by touching its keys—that is, that the nature of the keyboard dictates the progress of the composition. If the canzona had its origins in a generic vocal idiom, and the sonata was rooted in the sound of instruments, the toccata was rooted in the idiom of the keyboard. To some extent, this is apparent in the toccatas of Merulo: these pieces consist primarily of chordal frameworks, elaborated through diminution-style ornamentation (see example 8 and audio 8 on Fulcrum).[25]

There is widespread agreement among scholars today that most professional keyboard players in early modern Italy played both organ and harpsichord, and that the vast majority of keyboard music was written for either instrument. This underscores a truism of performance practice in early European classical music: while we might imagine an "authentic" performance on a "correct" instrument, players most often used the instrumental equipment that they had. However, as in most keyboard music of the late sixteenth century, this piece can be executed on either harpsichord or organ. It was up to the performer to execute the toccata in the manner that would sound best on each instrument.

This, however, was no small task. The differences between organs and harpsichords were significant, notwithstanding the obvious similarities of their player interface: the keyboard. The organ produces sound through the passing of air through pipes, while the harpsichord contains plectra that pluck the instrument's strings. In its method of sound production, as well as the quality and timbre of that sound, the harpsichord is closer to the lute than it is to the organ. Girolamo Diruta, who published a monumental treatise on organ playing (two parts, 1593 and 1609), devoted only a short passage to describing the distinction between performance on the organ and performance on the harpsichord, but that passage is significant. In particular, Diruta noted that the performance of chords on the two instruments was quite different. In answer to the question, "Why is it that many organists do not succeed in playing serious music on quilled instruments as well as they do on the organ?" Diruta addresses the idiomatic properties of the harpsichord—especially its quick decay:

> When you play a breve or semibreve on the organ, do you not hear the entire sound without striking the key more than one time? But when you play such a note on a quilled instrument more than half the sound is lost. So it is necessary to compensate for such a defect by lightly striking the key many times with quickness and dexterity of the hand.[26]

Further, Diruta explained that the harpsichord "should be played in a lively way so that the harmony is not lost, and it should be adorned with the *tremolo* and elegant *accenti*."[27] Arpeggiation, ornamentation, and the restriking of keys were essential aspects of harpsichord performance.

Thus, despite the fact that the *notation* of organ music was the same as that of harpsichord music, their manners of *execution* were substantially different. The performance style that Diruta described reached a new height in 1615, when Girolamo Frescobaldi published his first volume of toccatas and variation sets. The title page of this book specified the harpsichord alone as the intended instrument—*not* harpsichord or organ. (In 1628, when the volume was reprinted, the title page allowed for either instrument, but that does not negate the composer's initial impulse to single out the harpsichord as the ideal medium for these works.) The introduction to the volume, printed first in 1615 and revised and expanded in 1616, presents important information on harpsichord performance during this period. Among other important instructions, Frescobaldi indicates, notwithstanding their notation, "Let the beginnings of the toccatas be done slowly, and arpeggiated: and in the ties, or dissonances, as also in the middle of the work they will be struck together, in order not to leave the instrument empty: which striking will be repeated at the pleasure of the player."[28] Players must respond to the nature of the specific instrument in front of them. How quickly do the notes decay? How many times can or should they be restruck and ornamented to sustain the sound and emphasize the harmony? How long and how elaborately should each chord be rolled? In referring to "the beginnings of the toccatas," Frescobaldi called attention to passages like the opening of example 9, in which the sparse notation belies the complex realization that he had in mind. Note the extent to which the player in audio 9 embellishes the chords; this is done in a manner entirely in keeping with the historical evidence about Frescobaldi's performance practices. You can hear the harpsichordist seeming to "discover" the sounds of his instrument, responding to its sonic properties as he plays.

As with performances of Marini's violin compositions, the details of realization of the piece must be determined by the player in the moment of performance and in response to the tactile and sonic properties of the instrument. Indeed, Frescobaldi emphasizes the idiomatic nature of his toccatas in his letter of dedication to Don Fernando Gonzaga, printed in the same volume of toccatas, in which he writes that he had composed these pieces *sopra i tasti* ("upon the keyboard"). In this depiction, the act of playing or improvising had prompted him to compose, and he was guided in his composition by the physical construction and sounds of the instrument.

CONCLUSION

Rather than using their instruments to imitate the sounds of voices, many composers of the early seventeenth century saw the potential of instruments to lead them in new and exciting musical directions. Like natural philosophers such as Galileo, who used scientific instruments to explore the world around them, these composers harnessed their intimate knowledge of their instruments to act in an exploratory manner. Their music simulates the process of invention and discovery, assuming a posture of improvisation and invention on the spur of the moment, even as it continued to draw on actual improvisational practices. As artisanship came to be valued alongside literate traditions, users and players of instruments were increasingly valued by the learned and noble classes; the collections of curiosities that they amassed are paralleled by the collections of musical curiosities in the published music of Marini and others. Far from merely imitating their counterparts working in the genres of song and opera, instrumental composers embraced their medium with new boldness, finding their virtuosity and their expressive voices within the objects in their hands.

The ideas in this essay are drawn from Rebecca Cypess, Curious and Modern Inventions: Instrumental Music as Discovery in Galileo's Italy *(Chicago: University of Chicago Press, 2016).*

NOTES

1. Elam Rotem, "Artusi," Early Music Sources, accessed September 13, 2020, https://www.earlymusicsources.com/youtube/artusi.

2. Tom Huizenga, "Talk Like An Opera Geek: Arias, Odds And Ends," NPR, January 25, 2012, https://www.npr.org/sections/deceptivecadence/2012/01/25/145833505/talk-like-an-opera-geek-arias-odds-and-ends.

3. Rebecca Cypess, "'Esprimere la voce humana': Connections between Vocal and Instrumental Music by Italian Composers of the Early Seventeenth Century," *Journal of Musicology* (2010): 181–233, https://hcommons.org/deposits/objects/hc:20306/datastreams/CONTENT/content.

4. On the notion of scientific instruments as vehicles of discovery, see Jean-François Gauvin, "Instruments of Knowledge," in *The Oxford Handbook of Philosophy in Early Modern Europe*, ed. Desmond M. Clarke and Catherine Wilson (Oxford: Oxford University Press, 2011), 315–37, especially 331–33.

5. See Eileen Reeves, *Galileo's Glassworks: The Telescope and the Mirror* (Cambridge, MA: Harvard University Press, 2009); and Antoni Malet, "Early Conceptualizations of the Telescope as an Optical Instrument," *Early Science and Medicine* 10, no. 2 (2005): 237–62. An essential volume on the idea of artisan-ship and instrumentality in the early modern era is Pamela H. Smith, *The Body of the Artisan: Art and Experience in the Scientific Revolution* (New York: Routledge, 2004).

6. Eileen Reeves, *Painting the Heavens: Art and Science in the Age of Galileo* (Princeton, NJ: Princeton University Press, 1997).

7. In this context, it is important to mention the practice of basso continuo, chordal accompaniment using keyboard or plucked-string instruments such as lutes, which provided the backbone of ensemble music throughout the seventeenth and eighteenth centuries. The topic of basso continuo as an art dependent on both musical context and the performer's cultivated "instincts" and habits at the instrument is one that lies outside the scope of this study. For an overview of basso continuo in Italy, see Giulia Nuti, *The Performance of Italian Basso Continuo: Style in Keyboard Accompaniment in the Seventeenth and Eighteenth Centuries* (Aldershot, UK: Ashgate, 2007).

8. As Andrew Dell'Antonio has written, "While it is easy for us to accept

contemporary writers' neglect of instrumental music as a sign that such music was not held in high esteem, it is also crucial to analyze the *musical* roots of the *seconda prattica*, to understand how the theories relate to actual compositional praxis." Andrew Dell'Antonio, *Syntax, Form, and Genre in Sonatas and Canzonas, 1621–1635* (Lucca: Libreria Musicale Italiana, 1997), 295.

9. Wendy Powers, "Violin Makers: Nicolò Amati (1596–1684) and Antonio Stradivari (1644–1737)," The Met, October 2003, https://www.metmuseum.org/toah/hd/strd/hd_strd.htm.

10. The Met, "Cornetto in A," 1575; ivory, gilt (22 1/2 × 1 1/4 × 1 1/4 in.), Funds from various donors, 1952, 52.96.1, https://www.metmuseum.org/art/collection/search/503951; Wendy Powers, "The Development of the Recorder," The Met, October 2003, https://www.metmuseum.org/toah/hd/recd/hd_recd.htm; Will Kimball, "Trombone History: 17th Century (1601–1625)," Kimball Trombone, accessed September 13, 2020, http://kimballtrombone.com/trombone-history-timeline/17th-century-1601-1625/; College of Arts and Sciences, "Early Music Instrument Database: Shawm (Renaissance)," Case Western Reserve University, accessed September 13, 2020, https://caslabs.case.edu/medren/renaissance-instruments/shawm-renaissance/.

11. On instrumentation in the music of Gabrieli and his contemporaries, see Jeffery T. Kite-Powell, "Large Ensembles," in *A Performer's Guide to Renaissance Music*, 2nd ed., ed. Jeffery T. Kite-Powell (Bloomington: Indiana University Press, 2007), 250–54; and James Tyler, "Mixed Ensembles," in *A Performer's Guide to Renaissance Music*, 238–49. On organ accompaniment of polyphonic works, see Jack Ashworth and Paul O'Dette, "Proto-Continuo," in *A Performer's Guide to Renaissance Music*, 225–37; as well as Gregory S. Johnston, "Polyphonic Keyboard Accompaniment in the Early Baroque: An Alternative to Basso Continuo," *Early Music* 26, no. 1 (Feb. 1998): 51–64.

12. See Gregory Barnett, "Form and Gesture: Canzona, Sonata, and Concerto," in *The Cambridge History of Seventeenth-Century Music*, ed. Tim Carter and John Butt (Cambridge: Cambridge University Press, 2005), 482.

13. See Liza Malamut, "Higher, Faster, Louder? Applying Historical Brass Techniques to Modern Performances of Gabrieli's Music," *International Trombone Association Journal* 46, no. 4 (October, 2018): 37–41.

14. "Voi havete a sapere co[m]e tutti li instrumenti musicali sono rispetto & co[mp]aratione ala voce humana ma[n]cho degni p[er] tanto noi si afforzeremo da q[ue]lla i[m]parare & imitarla; onde tu potresti dire co[m]e sara possibile conciosia cosa che essa proferisce ogni parlare dil che no[n] credo che dito flauto mai sia simile ad essa humana voce & io te rispondo che cosi come il degno & p[er]fetto dipintor imita ogni cosa creata ala natura con la

variation di colori cosi con tale instrumento di fiato & corde potrai imitare el proferire che fa la humana voce." Silvestro Ganassi, *Opera intitulata fontegara la quale i[n]segna a sonare di flauto cho[n] tutta l'arte opportuna a e\u00dfo i[n] strumento massime il diminuire il quale sara utile ad ogni instrumento di fiato et chorde: et a[n]chora a chi si dileta di canto, co[m]posto per Sylvestro di Gana\u00dfi dal fo[n]tego sonator d[e] la Ill[ustris]sima S[ignoria] D[i] V[enetia]* (Venice: Ganassi, 1535), 2–3. My translation. For more on the connections between song and natural speech in the sixteenth century, see, for example, Anthony Rooley, "Ficino, and the Supremacy of Poetry Over Music," in *Le concert des voix et des instruments à la Renaissance: Actes du XXXIVe colloque internationale d'études humanistes Tours, Centre d'Études Superieures de la Renaissance, 1–11 juillet 1991,* ed. Jean Michel Vaccaro (Paris: CNRS, 1995), 51–6; and Howard Mayer Brown, "The Instrumentalist's Repertory in the Sixteenth Century," in *Le concert des voix et des instruments,* 21–32.

15. On the practices of listening in early modern Italy, see Andrew Dell'Antonio, *Listening as Spiritual Practice in Early Modern Italy* (Berkeley: University of California Press, 2011).

16. Andrew Dell'Antonio has explored the implications of the sonata/canzona terminology in the early seventeenth century in Dell'Antonio, *Syntax, Form, and Genre,* 252. Tarquinio Merula used the terms interchangeably in the title of his *Canzoni overo sonate concertate per chiesa e camera,* op. 12 (Venice: Vincenti, 1637).

17. See John Walter Hill, "The Emergence of Violin Playing into the Sphere of Art Music in Italy: *Compagnie di suonatori* in Brescia During the Sixteenth Century," in *Musica Franca: Essays in Honor of Frank A. D'Accone,* ed. Irene Alm, Alyson McLamore, and Colleen Reardon (Stuyvesant, NY: Pendragon Press, 1996), 333–366.

18. The literature on curiosities and Kunstkammern is vast, but two important sources are Lorraine Daston and Katharine Park, *Wonders and the Order of Nature, 1150–1750* (New York: Zone Books); Krzysztof Pomian, *Collectors and Curiosities: Paris and Venice, 1500–1800,* trans. Elizabeth Wiles-Portier (Cambridge, MA: Polity Press, 1990).

19. Wolfgang Wilhelm visited the court of the archduchess Isabella Clara Eugenia, ruler of the southern Netherlands, in 1623, and it was to Isabella that Marini dedicated the *Sonate.*

20. On the use of the *lira da braccio* to accompany poetry, see Blake Wilson, *Singing to the Lyre in Renaissance Italy* (Cambridge: Cambridge University Press, 2020), and Robert Nosow, "The Debate on Song in the *Accademia Fiorentina,*" *Early Music History* 21 (2002): 179–83.

21. Arne Spohr, "'Like an Earthly Paradise': Concealed Music and the Performance of the Other in Late Renaissance Pleasure Houses," in *Music and Diplomacy from the Early Modern Era to the Present*, ed. Rebekah Ahrendt and Damien Mahiet (New York: Palgrave Macmillan, 2014), 19–43.

22. Castello's biography has only recently begun to come into focus; see Rodolfo Baroncini, "Dario Castello e la formazione del musico a Venezia: nuovi documenti e nuove prospettive," *Recercare* 29 (2017): 53–100.

23. See Charles E. Brewer, The Instrumental Music of Schmeltzer, Biber, Muffat and Their Contemporaries (Aldershot: Ashgate, 2011).

24. See Lynette Bowring, "Orality, Literacy, and the Learning of Instruments: Professional Instrumentalists and Their Music in Early Modern Italy" (PhD diss., Rutgers University, 2017).

25. The diminution-style of ornamentation is discussed in Bruce Dickey, "Ornamentation in Early Seventeenth-Century Italian Music," in *A Performer's Guide to Seventeenth-Century Music*, ed. Stewart Cater, rev. and expanded by Jeffery T. Kite-Powell (Bloomington: Indiana University Press, 2012), 293–316, and Howard Mayer Brown, *Embellishing Sixteenth-Century Music* (London: Oxford University Press, 1976).

26. "Da che viene, che molti organist non li riesce il lor sonare musicale nelli istrumenti da penna come nell'organo?" "Quando sonate nell'organo una breve, over semibreve non si sente tutta la sua armonia senza percuotere più d'una volta il tasto: ma quando sonarete nell'istrumento da penna tal note li mancherà più della metà dell'armonia: bisogna dunque con la vivacità, & destrezza della mano supplire à tal mancamento con percuotere più volte il tasto leggiadramente." Girolamo Diruta, *Il Transilvano dialogo sopra il vero modo di sonar organi, et istromenti da penna* (Venice: Giacomo Vincenti, 1593), 1:12. Translated in Edward John Soehnlein, "Diruta on the Art of Keyboard Playing: An Annotated Translation and Transcription of *Il Transilvano*, Parts I (1593) and II (1609)" (PhD diss., University of Michigan, 1975), 1:54.

27. "sia sonata vivo, che non perda l'armonia; & che sia adornato con tremoli, e accenti leggiadri." See Diruta, *Il Transilvano dialogo.*

28. Translations of the various prefaces to Frescobaldi's publications are in Frederick Hammond, *Girolamo Frescobaldi: A Guide to Research* (New York: Garland, 1988), 186–90.

MACDOWELL'S VANISHING INDIANS

Dan Blim

To view all audio/visual examples referenced in this essay, please visit the open access version on Fulcrum at https://doi. org/10.3998/mpub.12063224.

I encountered this topic somewhat accidentally. I was doing some general background reading about the politics of borrowing and nationalism in turn-of-the-century US classical music. Not knowing much about MacDowell, I decided to read a couple articles about him, but MacDowell was never meant to be my primary focus. Reading, I was intrigued by the multiple ways scholars interpreted his borrowing of Native American music in his "Indian" Suite for Orchestra. Indulging my curiosity, I listened to a couple of MacDowell's other works that contained the word "Indian," the two works I discuss in this article. Examining them, I was struck by both their similarity of form, namely a central quotation "framed" by other music, and also by the difference in moods. Upon further study, this seemed to be the traditional "gap" in the literature; neither work had attracted much attention. The clarity of the borrowing, compared to the more complex Indian Suite, made these an appealing subject. As I then read more in American Studies and Native American Studies, I could see this concept of the "vanishing Indian" at work in both.

In many ways this essay was a departure for me. It's more centered on close musical analysis, and from an era and genre I haven't studied much. But the central questions about how musical borrowing works and the political meanings of music and identity are central to much of my research. Toward the end of the essay, I was able to do some visual analysis on the cover—having a background in art history, it's always gratifying to do that work. The connections made to literature of the time were suggested by colleagues in an interdisciplinary workshop, further proof that reading and conversing broadly can be extremely beneficial.

In the summer of 1893, millions of Americans flocked to Chicago to attend the Chicago World's Fair. One of the most popular attractions was the Midway, a line of carnival attractions that featured a number of international and exoticized folk villages. Included here was a Native American village, where several tribes displayed artifacts and performed music and dances. While undoubtedly offering visitors a chance to engage in some form of colonialist tourism, historian David Beck has argued that the fair provided Native Americans one of their earliest opportunities to self-represent for audiences familiar only with the caricatures featured in Buffalo Bill's traveling shows.[1] The exhibit also generated interest in anthropological ethnography for some visitors, including Frances Densmore, who first encountered Native American music there.

Densmore was not the only visitor whose encounter sparked an interest in Native American music. In June, composer Antonín Dvořák visited the fair; and in December 1893, he premiered his ninth symphony in New York City. Accompanying the premiere, Dvořák penned an essay in the *New York Herald*, repeating earlier suggestions that African American songs might serve US composers looking for nationalist source material but now suggesting

Native American melodies for that same purpose. Michael Pisani has astutely noted that while Dvořák's promotion of African American music has since overshadowed his similar promotion of Native American music, it was his interest in this music that had the greater immediate impact.[2]

Not long after Dvořák's pronouncement, a so-called Indianist movement emerged among Euro-American composers, placing Native American subjects at the fore of US musical nationalism. This movement spanned a few decades, from about 1890 to 1920. It was not formally organized, but rather reflected a growing interest in the collection, setting, and imagining of Native American melodies, aided by the work of ethnographers and anthropologists. Composers took varied approaches. Some had direct contact with Native Americans, such as Arthur Nevin, who spent two summers with the Blackfoot tribe, and Charles Wakefield Cadman, who gave lecture-recitals with Cherokee-Creek princess Tsianina Redfeather. Others relied on published transcriptions. Composers Arthur Farwell and Charles Wakefield Cadman were especially active and set Native American songs as art songs; Farwell also founded the Wa-Wan Press, which became a central publication venue for Indianist music. Operas, too, became popular vehicles for developing romanticized stories on Native American subjects, including Cadman's *Shanewis*, which appeared at the Metropolitan Opera, Nevin's *Poia*, and Charles Sanford Skilton's *Kalopin*. Finally, composers like Edward MacDowell and Amy Beach used Native American melodies as thematic material for a wide range of instrumental works.

In many ways, MacDowell was a marginal figure to this movement. He composed very few works using Native American themes and never had any direct contact with Native American music. Moreover, he was quite skeptical of musical nationalism, an ideal other Indianist composers embraced.[3] MacDowell felt that blatant attempts to elevate US composers were politically rather than aesthetically motivated, and he feared that the quality of

US compositions would suffer if not aspiring to be "universalist" in nature (i.e., equal to European masterworks). Although such misgivings yielded a minimal engagement with Native American music, Michael Pisani attributes the success of the Indianist movement in large part to the participation of MacDowell, who was the preeminent US composer of the day.

MacDowell premiered his first and most famous Indianist work, the *Second Suite for Orchestra*, also known as the *Indian Suite*, in 1896. MacDowell's *Indian Suite* has been the subject of much musicological analysis, much of it focused on the relationship between Western-European classical music and Native American music. Richard Crawford and Tara Browner focus specifically on the fourth movement of the *Suite*, marked "Dirge." Crawford, elucidating MacDowell's own critical position on nationalism, finds in the use of Native American music a specifically American source for writing universalist music.[4] In particular, Crawford describes how a quoted Native American melody is treated developmentally, with late romantic Wagnerian harmonies and a tonally ambiguous sense of mystery. Browner takes MacDowell to task for his borrowing strategies and, agreeing with Crawford, asserts that his Western-European musical sources supply the emotions, while "his cut-and-paste adaptation of the [Native American] song nullifies any innate anguish it might possess."[5] Both Crawford and Browner locate MacDowell's interests squarely in the Western-European compositional approach rather than in the Native American source material, which provides mere thematic fodder for the movement or a nationalistic link for writing universalist symphonic music. Pisani, examining the *Suite* as a whole, agrees with Crawford, positing that the quotations largely serve to "anchor the work in the geography of America, while lending it a degree of authenticity."[6] Yet Pisani finds that the Western-European classical music that surrounds the quotations is not simply universal but uses standard exotic devices of modal harmonies and narrative structures to signify Indianness, a process Pisani calls "intonation."[7]

The most extensive treatment of the *Suite* is given by Kara Anne Gardner, who offers a compelling reading of the work as embodying "simultaneous desire and repulsion" toward Native Americans. Gardner frames the encounter between Western-European and Native American musics as an implicit battle. This battle, she argues, is narratively structured within the work: foreshadowed in the first movement ("Legend"), fought in the third ("In War-Time"), lamented in the fourth ("Dirge"), and finally unsettled in the fifth ("Village Festival"), which closes the work with a celebration that "most reflects the jumble of confused emotion MacDowell feels for the Native Americans who are the subject of his piece."[8] Gardner then contextualizes this battle within the conflicting ideologies surrounding Native Americans at the time, reflecting the "wild" and "noble savage" tropes common to US culture. The "wild" Native American subject offered a primitiveness to be feared and contrasted with modernity's civilization, while the "noble" subject offered a nostalgic freedom that countered MacDowell's anxieties about modernity.

MacDowell went on to complete two more works on Native American subjects—two piano miniatures as part of Americana suites: "From an Indian Lodge" from *Woodland Sketches*, published that same year in 1896, and "Indian Idyl" from *New England Idyls*, published in 1902. These works, unlike the *Indian Suite*, have attracted relatively little attention. Lawrence Gilman, Alan Levy, and Douglas Bomberger all mention these other works in their biographical studies of MacDowell, but only briefly in descriptions of their respective larger piano suites within which they were published. The Native American subject matter is absent entirely from Gilman's mention, and Bomberger only characterizes it as "nostalgic," similar to the other piano character pieces.[9] Levy goes slightly further, calling "From an Indian Lodge" "a most sincere tribute" to Native Americans, but he discusses "Indian Idyl" merely in terms of a clear form and contrasting moods.[10] These two works, in other words, invite further analysis. But simply applying scholars' arguments about the *Indian Suite* to these two piano miniatures will not suffice. Further analysis is necessary precisely because of the ways they contrast with Mac-Dowell's more famous Indianist work.

How do these works compare with the *Indian Suite*? Unlike the treatment of the quotation in the "Dirge" movement, the melody is not merely ancillary to a Western compositional approach, as Browner's and Crawford's analyses suggest; in both works, the quoted melody is central to the structure of the piece. Rather than Browner's "cut and paste" metaphor, the two piano works use Western-European music to frame the quotation, placing the emphasis on the quoted material. I find Gardner's culturally situated analysis useful, but the works forego the epic battle narrative, settling on a more purely nostalgic view of the Native American subject. Nevertheless, they still feature a complex relationship to their Native American subjects, one that reflected the shifting position of Native Americans within the American imagination at the time. Specifically, I argue these works musically align with the emerging concept of what historians call the "vanishing Indian." In the following, I provide first an explanation of the concept of the "vanishing Indian," then offer a close reading of both works within this framework.

THE "VANISHING INDIAN"

In addition to staging Native American cultures, the Chicago World's Fair of 1893 was also the site of Frederick Jackson Turner's landmark address "The Significance of the Frontier in American History." Turner began his remarks by quoting the 1890 census, which observed the disappearance of a Western frontier line of settlement, marking, in Turner's words, the end of a historical era. Turner repeatedly associates Native Americans with that frontier line of unsettled land, yet his position on the relationship between Native Americans and Euro-Americans is harder to pin down. At times, he views them as antithetical opposing forces: "The effect of the Indian frontier as a consolidating agent in our history is important. . . . The Indian was a common danger, demanding united action."[11] Yet elsewhere he marks Native American cultures as necessary, transformative forces in the creation of a new American population:

> The frontier is the line of most rapid and effective Americanization. The wilderness masters the colonist. It finds him a European in dress, industries, tools, modes of travel, and thought. It takes him from the railroad car and puts him in the birch canoe. It strips off the garments of civilization and arrays him in the hunting shirt and the moccasin. It puts him in the log cabin of the Cherokee and Iroquois and runs an Indian palisade around him. Before long he has gone to planting Indian corn and plowing with a sharp stick; he shouts the war cry and takes the scalp in orthodox Indian fashion. In short, at the frontier the environment is at first too strong for the man. He must accept the conditions which it furnishes, or perish, and so he fits himself into the Indian clearings and follows the Indian trails. Little by little he transforms the wilderness; but the outcome is not the old Europe, not simply the development of Germanic germs, any more than the first phenomenon was a case of reversion to the Germanic mark. The fact is, that here is a new product that is American.[12]

In other words, European settlers had to go through a phase of adopting Native American ways to shed their European traditions and become newly American.

In both cases, however, Turner places these relationships between Euro-Americans and Native Americans squarely in the past. He frequently conflates the disappearance of the frontier with the disappearance of the Native tribes (some of whom were, at that very moment, encamped on the Midway). He writes, "Long before the pioneer farmer appeared on the scene, primitive Indian life had passed away."[13] Turner's choice of verb here—*passed* away—is telling in its literal passivity. Turner asserts what American studies scholar Alan Trachtenberg calls "the 'vanishing race' theory," which "dominated all thinking about Native Americans until quite recently, the idea that the indigenes of the continent would disappear as a matter of natural course."[14] In her book *Going Native: Indians in the American Cultural Imagination*, Shari Huhndorf further demonstrates how the 1893 fair sent conflicting messages about Native Americans: depicted as savage, exotic, and inferior in order to celebrate the technological progress of white settlers, while also serving as a quintessentially American symbol of its own past, a preserved historical artifact.[15]

The fair came on the heels of a series of governmental actions that further shifted US views toward Native Americans. By the end of the nineteenth century, the long and violent war waged by the westward-expanding Euro-Americans against Native American tribes was drawing to a close. The Dawes Act of 1887 broke up Native American territories, permitted the US government to redistribute land, and pushed for the assimilation of Native Americans into US society. The bloody massacre three years later at Wounded Knee Creek in South Dakota effectively marked the end of Native American armed resistance. These events suggest how Native Americans, in their defeat, seemed to "vanish" as a threat to Euro-American settlers either through assimilation or death. Thus, in the Euro-American imagination, Native American archetypes were no longer considered a threat and could be appropriated as nostalgic figures rather than a living oppositional force. Doing so, moreover, erased the unsavory role Euro-Americans played in that vanishing.

Given the pervasiveness of the vanishing race theory in his time, Edward MacDowell's attitudes toward Native Americans and their music makes sense. MacDowell made only a few comments about Native Americans in his writing. As Douglas Bomberger notes in his recent biography of the composer, by 1891 at the latest,

MacDowell had expressed an interest in Native American music and his student, Henry Gilbert, brought him a copy of Theodore Baker's 1882 dissertation "Über die Musik der noramerikanischen Wilden," which included a number of transcriptions.[16] MacDowell shared Baker's concern that these melodies would vanish and saw *Über die Musik* as a form of cultural preservation through transcriptions not unlike the projects Cecil Sharp, Bela Bartok, and other Europeans were beginning around the same time. Unlike other collectors, however, MacDowell often stressed the universal value of this music rather than folklike nationalistic value.[17] Yet MacDowell did differentiate these melodies from Western-European classical music at other times. He felt the presence of quoted melodies in the *Indian Suite* lent it an air of savage authenticity and remarked that most performances disappointed him as too genteel.[18] Such comments echo Turner's depiction of the Native American as a threatening foreign force. Still elsewhere, MacDowell adopts language more in line with the recent shift toward the vanishing Indian. In response to Dvořák, MacDowell remarked, "What Negro melodies have to do with Americanism still remains a mystery to me. Why cover a beautiful thought with the badge of whilom slavery rather than with the stern but at least manly and free rudeness of the North American Indian?"[19] With this division, slavery remains a blight on the national character while the brutal military campaign against Native Americans has been erased, along with the savageness of the Native American. This nostalgic view of the Native American was much in line with the "vanishing Indian" and, I argue, shaped MacDowell's musical treatment of the subject in the two piano miniatures, to which I turn now for a close analysis.

MACDOWELL'S INDIANIST MINIATURES

When considering musical quotations, meaning is constructed not simply by examining what is quoted, but how it is quoted as well.

V.

From an Indian Lodge.

Example 1. Edward MacDowell, "From an Indian Lodge."

Example 1 continued

Attending to aspects of form, dynamics, harmony, and meter, as well as to any alterations to the quotation, helps the listener understand the nuances of musical meaning. "From an Indian Lodge," from *Woodland Sketches*, is cast in a ternary ABA form; the first A and central B sections each quote a melody borrowed from Baker's collection (see examples 1 and 2; see example 1 audio on Fulcrum). MacDowell

Lied der Brotherton-Indianer.

Hi tu e oo ha ha hi tu e oo ha ha ha ha ha ha ha ha ha ha ha

Hi tu e - a tut-t - t - tut-t - tut-t - t - t - tut

Wa - a ich e - e wa - - a

ich e - e Wa-a ich Wa - a ich.

Example 2. Melodies from Theodore Baker, quoted in "From an Indian Lodge."[20]

seems to conjure up the idea of "manly and free rudeness" at the outset, where MacDowell instructs the performer to play "sternly and with great emphasis." But MacDowell marks the central portion "mournfully," quite possibly mourning the vanishing of the Native American race—a feeling compounded by the ritardando at the end of the section. The middle section is further demarcated by dynamic contrast—the opening fortissimo drops to piano for the quoted melody, suggesting the evocation of Native American life is either kept at some distance, or kept as an object of somber reverence, before the crashing fortissimo of the conclusion insists upon the finality of the Native American's death. MacDowell also doubles the quoted melody in octaves, specifying that it is at first to be heard in the lower notes for sixteen measures, then in the upper notes for the last eight measures of the quotation. The emphasized lower notes would appear to be in keeping with the masculine character of the piece. The shift of emphasis in the final phrase—which is almost identical to the first eight measures—suggests a kind of displaced echo, in keeping with the sense of distance and loss.

To borrow Pisani's term, the music intones "Indianness" through several stock tropes. First, MacDowell opens the piece by harmonizing a borrowed major-key melody in a minor key, creating modal mixture—a common exoticizing trope—by preserving the melody's raised sixth.[21] The central section limits the harmonization to two notes, played on the second beat of each bar, over an open fifth on C and G. The repeating open fifths imply a drone, which frequently suggest the pastoral and the exotic, while the steady rhythm simulates a drumbeat to be performed "detached throughout," furthering its role as a separate percussive accompaniment rather than a harmonization of the melody. At the same time, MacDowell subtly Europeanizes this melody. The original melody is twenty-eight bars: a repeating seven-bar phrase, followed by a fourteen-bar phrase. In MacDowell's hands, not only is the repeat ignored, but the final notes are elongated to produce three regular eight-bar phrases. Moreover, MacDowell slightly alters the rhythm in the third-to-last bar of the quotation and the melody in the second-to-last bar. These alterations make the final eight-bar phrase mirror exactly the first eight-bar phrase and thereby form a small-scale ternary (ABA) form within the quotation.

While the quotations offer a stern and somber portrait of the Native American subject, MacDowell also adds four bars of music at the end of the first A section: a highly theatrical chord progression with tremolo, which is repeated at the close of the work. The theatricality of these brief passages perhaps relates to the title of

VI.

INDIAN IDYL.

Alone by the wayward flame
She weaves broad wampum skeins
While afar through the summer night
Sigh the wooing flutes' soft strains.

New England Idyls   8.

Example 3. Edward MacDowell, "Indian Idyl."

Example 3 continued

Example 3 continued

the work "From an Indian Lodge." Indian lodges were fraternal organizations that had been around since the early nineteenth century but grew in popularity at the end of that century among middle-class Euro-American males, with up to one-fifth of all men belonging to a fraternal organization.[22] The organizations provided a sense of unity for white males feeling threatened by changes in a modern America, offering a model of manliness and, somewhat ironically, racial purity by hearkening to an idealized America of the past. MacDowell's music resonates with this practice with its stern, stoic nature and simple, unadorned presentation. And the theatricality of the musical frame around the quotations suggests the music performs the same sort of reimagining of Native American subjects that these lodges undertook.

In light of its theatrical frame and denotative title, the subject of this work is not simply Native American, but a reenactment of an imagined past. MacDowell in fact returns to the same tremolo chord progression to conclude the tenth and final piece in *Woodland Sketches*, fittingly titled "Told at Sunset." The gesture here seems to acknowledge MacDowell's own desire to tell a tale about Native Americans in "From an Indian Lodge," a tale told at the perceived "sunset" of their existence. The quotations of melodies are preserved by MacDowell yet are subtly Westernized through their reenactment here and given the solemn reverence of a historical tableau, where the crashing final chord lowers the curtain on the performance and in turn on the lives of the Native American subjects.

"Indian Idyl" from *New England Idyls* resembles "From an Indian Lodge" formally—it is also cast in a ternary form and similarly highlights a quoted Native American melody within the central B section (see example 3; see example 3 audio on Fulcrum). But the mood here is quite different: a reverie of an imagined, idyllic Native American past made evident at the outset where MacDowell instructs the performer to play "lightly, naively." The piece opens with a breezy four-bar phrase, played twice with gently chromatic harmonies and a laugh-like gesture at the end, giving the work the intimate, nostalgic feeling of a parlor song. Finally, the phrase is heard a third time, expanded to six bars, moving from F to A minor before a half-cadence at the end on the dominant of F. But this cadence is sharply broken off by a two-bar unison phrase centered around the open fifth of the notes E and B, similar to the unison open fifth call that opened "From an Indian Lodge." The music's function is similar too, commanding the listener's attention with a ceremonial herald, for what follows is the central B section where the quoted melody is given pride of place.

The central B section is again contrasted with the preceding A section. The modulation from F major to A major suggests that this music is distant from the opening phrases, and yet the hints of A minor in the earlier music help make this distance feel more familiar and accessible. The accompaniment dispenses with the parlor song harmonies, settling on a drone of open fifths—again, a stock trope of pastoral, folk, and exoticized music—though slightly distorted, as it is spread across two registers. At the same time, the accompaniment shifts through a hemiola to create a temporary feeling of duple meter, even subtly suggesting the same type of regular percussive drum beat heard in "From an Indian Lodge." This duple meter again detaches from the melody, where the triplets create a momentary sense of triple meter. The harmonic displacement of the dotted end of the phrase, from the downbeat in the first phrase to the second beat in the second phrase, further confuses the metrical sensibility. Finally, the use of the damper and soft pedals—marked "pianississimo (ppp)"—throughout this section creates a sonic haze to emphasize the dreamy distance that envelops the quoted material. If "From an Indian Lodge" sought to remember Native American culture through a fictional theatricality, this work couches Native American culture within a hazy, imagined reverie. The connection of this reverie to the "vanishing Indian" ideology is made more concrete at the end of the B section, as MacDowell directs the player to play "gradually dying out" and "with pathos," expressing not only the musical emotion but perhaps also a knowing attitude of passive sadness toward the dying out of the Native American culture the musical quotation ostensibly represents.

Following the quotation, a variation of the opening music is heard again, but something is off. First, it enters in the wrong key—A, the key of the dreamy central part, not F. And second, the harmonization undercuts the melody by slowing down and cadencing on an arresting A minor chord, held with a fermata. There is a tinge of irrevocable sadness at this moment, something the music cannot dispel.

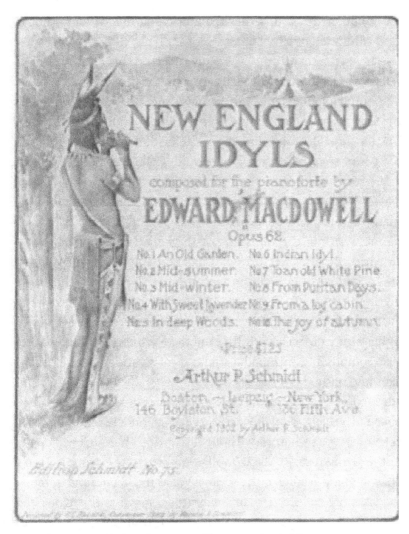

Example 4. Cover of Edward MacDowell's *New England Idyls*.

The reprise of the A music, now heard in the correct key, still feels unable to capture the lighthearted qualities heard earlier: harmonies are more expressively chromatic, the laughing gestures at the end occur on the wrong pitches, suggesting A major, and at the very end, the triplets from the quoted melody return briefly. Whether or not one hears this as some sort of subtle acknowledgement of guilt, the reverie nevertheless unsettles the music that follows and is not so easily forgotten or left behind.

This is a far cry from the "manly rudeness" of "From an Indian Lodge." Indeed, MacDowell affixed a poetic epigram to the score, describing a lonely female Indian, weaving by the fire "while afar through the summer night / sigh the wooing flutes' soft strains." The images of female domesticity and distant romantic music suit the parlor song reimagining here quite well. "Indian Idyl" reflects a different aspect of the "vanishing Indian" ideology. In his book *Shades of Hiawatha: Staging Indians, Making Americans 1890–1930*, Alan Trachtenberg observes the "inseparability" of Indians and nature, writing "the vanishing of the native often took the paradoxical and perverse form of a heightened visibility in Western landscape painting and photography. . . . Even when they were present, natives often remained in some important respect invisible, part of the scenery, natural objects."[23] Musicologist Beth Levy, in her study of music and the American frontier, similarly notes that composers continued a tradition of treating "Native Americans and nature as a single entity—an unspoiled geography to be admired or a fearsome obstacle to be conquered. . . . Their music encoded a celebration of westward expansion wherein they could celebrate Indian heroes without disrupting the tragic trajectory of the 'dying race.'"[24] MacDowell's embrace of this trope within a New England setting, rather than a Western US one, and in music that is more reflective than celebratory, suggests this trope was pervasive and adaptable to various forms of imagining a US past or national identity.

The cover of the collection of *New England Idyls* seems to highlight the conflation of the "vanishing Indian" with nature (see example 4). While most of the works in the collection suggest natural imagery, "Indian Idyl" is the only one to take on a Native American subject. Why would this image serve to stand for the whole collection? The conflation of Native Americans with nature and with US national identity surely offers some reasons. But it also captures a nostalgic sensibility. The male figure is rendered nonthreatening and passive, turned away from the reader, playing his flute—perhaps the very same "wooing soft strains" from the epigraph—and gazing off into the distance. The rest of the image is one of nature, an imagined "pre-civilization" America, which subtly incorporates the Native American as part of the landscape. The shape of the teepee in the distance echoes the distant hills, while the Native American in the foreground is coupled with the tall trees, and the fringe on his clothing blurs indistinctly into the tall grass. Thus the Native American subject becomes part of not just any landscape but a specifically New England landscape, a revision that moves the Native American from the wild frontier and into the precolonial heart of America's founding. The viewer can thus safely identify with the Native American figure, looking not only with him at the teepee from a lonely distance but looking at him with that same lonely distance from the present.

CONCLUSION: HISTORY'S VANISHING VOICES

"Indian Idyl" and "From an Indian Lodge" set out to capture seemingly vanishing Native American music through their quotations and intonations. In doing so, they also preserved the cultural attitudes of the time among Euro-Americans, which we can understand through an analysis of MacDowell's setting. Both works present the Native American subject as an object of passive remembrance, whether the stoic lamentation of "From an Indian Lodge" or the romantic natural reverie of "Indian Idyl." Both share a tension between maintaining distance with the Native American as an "exotic other" and allowing an identification with the subject. This tension informs the way that musical contrasts in each work preserve distance and otherness, the way quoted melodies are subtly tamed and westernized through balanced phrase structures and tonal harmonic progressions to allow identification, and the way ternary forms safely "capture" the Native American subject within a Western—or even more specifically, a New England frame. In other words, it is MacDowell's voice we hear in this music, rather than the voice of the Native American subjects. And in various ways, that voice was vanishing too.

These tensions are characteristic of of what Philip Deloria calls "playing Indian."[25] Deloria describes a long history of "playing Indian" in US culture, but at the turn of the century, it was especially an exercise in nostalgia, marked by the closing of the frontier. By forcibly assimilating Native Americans into their culture, Euro-Americans could adopt them as ancestral markers of Americanness without sacrificing their own cultural dominance. Kara Anne Gardner adopts this same framework of "playing Indian" in her analysis of the *Indian Suite*, arguing that Native Americans presented for MacDowell a nostalgic, antimodernist figure tied to nature, which MacDowell preferred over the city. At the same time, she observes that in celebrating the pastness of the Native American, composers, writers, and artists "also reinforced the idea that the disappearance of native cultures was an inevitable part of the civilizing process."[26] Indeed, other scholars have posited that the "vanishing Indian" supplied a model for a late-nineteenth-century American nationalism brought about by specific, contemporary anxieties. Shari Huhndorf situates the "vanishing Indian" in the wake of enormous geographic expansion, a divisive Civil War, economic unrest and strikes, and waves of immigration from Asia and Eastern Europe, and argues that "Indians, now safely 'vanishing,' began to provide the symbols and myths upon which white Americans created a sense of historical authenticity."[27] In his study of early twentieth-century literature, Walter Benn Michaels similarly observes how Native Americans in novels offered a safe model for white cultural purity, choosing to die out rather than marry into white society: "It is because the Indian's sun was perceived as setting that he could become . . . a kind of paradigm for increasingly powerful American notions of ethnic identity and eventually for the idea of an ethnicity that could be threatened or defended."[28] Although MacDowell never embraced the idea of musical nationalism, and may not have consciously or even unconsciously harbored these feelings, his music nevertheless participated in a larger cultural movement that tied US identity to a nostalgic "vanishing" past.

In the years since, Indianist compositional voices like Mac-Dowell's have vanished somewhat themselves. Quite popular at the turn of the twentieth century, most of these works (with a few exceptions, like Dvořák's *Symphony No. 9*) remain outside the canon. Other sonic markers of the US have thrived in ways Indianist works have not, including Copland's sounds of Western frontiers and Duke Ellington's sounds of Harlem nightclubs. Why do certain images retain the power to serve as nationalist images, while others do not? Did the systematic erasure of Native Americans—the very act that allowed Euro-Americans to safely appropriate their image in their works—ultimately doom these works to feel increasingly obsolete and disconnected from a modern nation where Native Americans continue to be marginalized? Do their legacies of violent misappropriation make modern audiences uncomfortable?

Moreover, although MacDowell's *Indian Suite* has at least attracted scholarly attention, "From an Indian Lodge" and "Indian Idyl" have not, and it is worthwhile to ask why. Part of the reason may lie in their genre. Symphonic music has traditionally been coded as masculine,[29] a connotation borne out in the *Suite*'s bellicose and exciting character. In contrast, piano music, and in particular the piano-character piece, was a staple of domestic music making during the second half of the nineteenth century and would more likely have been played by women.[30] Perhaps Mac-Dowell's seemingly passive, nostalgic, and potentially feminized visions of US identity ceased to fit as the twentieth century continued.[31] Yet such works, played in middle-class parlors, surely helped to shape the popular imagination of Native Americans at the time, maybe even more powerfully than symphonic works and operas.

These are three very different vanishing acts: the violent

eradication of Native Americans and their culture, the gradual disappearance of Indianist music among US composers, and the absence of these piano works among scholarly discussions. Yet for the music historian, all deserve our attention. We must be attuned not only to voices that vanish but also to the processes by which they vanish. By listening closely to these two piano pieces, by refusing to let them vanish, I find they have much to say about their time, adding nuances to other scholarship about Indianist works. They demonstrate a need to confront the myths and truths that shaped US history.

NOTES

1. See chapter two of David Beck and Rosalyn R. LaPier, *City Indian: Native American Activism in Chicago, 1893–1934* (Lincoln: University of Nebraska Press, 2015), doi:10.2307/j.ctt1d98ch6.

2. Michael Pisani, *Imagining Native America in Music* (New Haven, CT: Yale University Press, 2005), 211, doi:10.12987/yale/9780300108934.001.0001.

3. See Richard Crawford, "Edward MacDowell: Musical Nationalism and an American Tone Poet," *Journal of the American Musicological Society* 49, no. 3 (Autumn 1996): 538–42, doi:10.2307/831771.

4. Crawford, "Edward MacDowell," 551.

5. Tara Browner, "'Breathing the Indian Spirit': Thoughts on Musical Borrowing and the 'Indianist' Movement," *American Music* 15, no. 3 (Autumn 1997): 270, doi:10.2307/3052325.

6. Pisani, *Imagining*, 204.

7. Pisani, 198–99.

8. Kara Anne Gardner, "Edward MacDowell, Antimodernism, and 'Playing Indian' in the *Indian Suite*," *Musical Quarterly* 87, no. 3 (Fall 2004): 401, https://doi.org/10.1093/musqtl/gdh016.

9. Lawrence Gilman, *Edward MacDowell: A Study* (New York: John Lane, 1909), 140–141 and 145; Douglas Bomberger, *MacDowell* (New York: Oxford University Press, 2013), 199–203, 247–48, doi:10.1093/acprof:osobl/9780199899296.001.0001.

10. Alan H. Levy, *Edward MacDowell: An American Master* (Lanham, MD: Scarecrow Press, 1998), 155–56 and 178.

11. Frederick Jackson Turner, "The Significance of the Frontier in American History," in *Annual Report of the American Historical Association: The Year 1893* (Washington, DC: Government Printing Office, 1894), 210.

12. Turner, "The Significance," 201

13. Turner, 209.

14. Alan Trachtenberg, *Shades of Hiawatha: Staging Indians, Making Americans, 1880–1930* (New York: Hill & Wang, 2004), 4.

15. See chapter 1 of Shari M. Huhndorf, *Going Native: Indians in the American Cultural Imagination* (Ithaca, NY: Cornell University Press, 2001).

16. Henry F. Gilbert, "Personal Recollections of Edward MacDowell," *New Music Review* 2 (November 1912), 496–97, cited in Bomberger, *MacDowell*, 194. See also Francis Brancaleone, "Edward MacDowell and Indian Motives," *American Music* 7, no. 4 (Winter, 1989): 359–81, specifically 359.

17. Levy, *Edward MacDowell*, 120.

18. Crawford, "Edward MacDowell," 551.

19. Gilman, *Edward MacDowell*, 84.

20. Theodore Baker, *On the Music of the North American Indians*, trans. Ann Buckley (New York: Da Capo Press, 1977), 75 and 78.

21. For more information on these tropes, see Ralph P. Locke, *Musical Exoticism: Images and Reflections* (New York: Cambridge University Press, 2009).

22. See Mark C. Carnes, *Secret Ritual and Manhood in Victorian America* (New Haven, CT: Yale University Press, 1989), 1; and Huhndorf, *Going Native*, 65–78.

23. Trachtenberg, *Shades of Hiawatha*, 193.

24. Beth E. Levy, *Frontier Figures: American Music and the Mythology of the American West* (Berkeley: University of California Press, 2012), 15, doi:10.1525/california/9780520267763.001.0001.

25. Philip J. Deloria, *Playing Indian* (New Haven, CT: Yale University Press, 1999).

26. Gardner, "Edward MacDowell," 417.

27. Huhndorf, *Going Native*, 22.

28. Walter Benn Michaels, *Our America: Nativism, Modernism, and Pluralism* (Durham, NC: Duke University Press, 1995), 38, https://doi.org/10.1215/9780822397434.

29. Christopher Small, *Musicking: The Meanings of Performing and Listening* (Middletown, CT: Wesleyan University Press, 1998), 171.

30. See chapter 1 of Craig H. Roell, *The Piano in America, 1890–1940* (Chapel Hill: University of North Carolina Press, 1989).

31. Bomberger has discussed MacDowell's reception in similar terms, noting that his sentiment was keenly mocked and feminized by successive modernist figures. See Bomberger, *MacDowell*, 290.

JENNY LIND AND THE MAKING OF MAINSTREAM AMERICAN POPULAR MUSIC

Julia Chybowski

As a musicologist, I study music in its historical contexts and am particularly interested in relationships between music and culture. In my research, writing, and teaching, I often focus on musicians in the United States who seem to be so embedded in culture that it is difficult to say whether they are reflecting culture or influencing it. Indeed, most popular music success stories from the history of the United States can be described by this cyclical relationship of music to culture. I am also interested in historical musical phenomena that have a legacy today. While Jenny Lind's mid-nineteenth century world is in many ways foreign to our twenty-first century lives, processes of mainstream media constructing "idealized" status of celebrity musicians is still happening—even though the media and technologies have changed. This essay about Jenny Lind's midnineteenth-century US concert tour is a case study for these ways of thinking about musics embedded in culture and the legacy of historical musical-cultural processes.

Sources and methods for this research include those that are common to historical musicology and cultural historians. Reading and interpreting primary source materials, such as newspaper advertisements for concerts and concert reviews, is fundamental. Digitized collections of nineteenth-century newspapers are making this type of historical research more efficient, and more sources are coming to light. However, even artifacts previously interpreted sometimes warrant revisiting, because scholars today can ask new questions of the sources and bring in additional critical lenses. Besides reading primary-source materials that mention music explicitly, a scholar of nineteenth-century music must also learn about expectations for gender, race, and class norms and ideals that influenced the reception of nineteenth-century musicians. This knowledge comes from interpretation of primary sources, as well as engagement with interdisciplinary scholarship. Lind's status as "ideal" grew from the cultural discourse about her singing voice as gendered, raced, and classed. These aspects of identity are also useful lenses of cultural interpretation that help us gain a more complete picture of Jenny Lind's embeddedness in mid-nineteenth-century US culture, as well as her appeal as a musical celebrity.

Tens of thousands of Americans flocked to greet Jenny Lind's steamship as it entered New York City's harbor in September of 1850.[1] This was owing to much advance publicity organized by P. T. Barnum, the professional showman and entertainment manager, who had arranged for her to travel to the United States from Europe for a concert tour. Lind, a professional singer by training who had recently retired from an operatic career in Europe, would become an early example of musical celebrity in the United States. However, not even her US manager, nor the others building the hype about her in the United States, had heard her sing. Hundreds of thousands would eventually hear her sing the parlor songs, folk music, hymns, and opera arias that were the popular music of mid-nineteenth-century America. Touring as the "Swedish Nightingale," she met tremendous popular success. At great expense, grand concert halls were constructed especially for her performances and to accommodate the huge crowds she drew.[2] Tickets to hear and see the Swedish Nightingale sold quickly, sometimes for as much as several hundred dollars.[3] And then there was the merchandising—it seems everyone tried to cash in on the sensation by selling Jenny Lind clothing, accessories, tonics, cosmetics, furniture, new varieties of garden melons, sheet music for her signature songs, and much more.[4] Her singing voice would become legendary, but the hype was about more than her voice.

In the era before recorded sound—when all music was necessarily live—contemporary print media played a major role in constructing the Swedish Nightingale phenomenon. US newspaper coverage of Jenny Lind surged as soon as Barnum arranged for her to travel to the United States. Newspaper attention remained obsessive during the concert tour. We might ask what education and other advantages in her life facilitated such rise to fame and look to her personal biography for explanations for her success, as other scholars have done,[5] but this essay approaches her popularity instead as a cultural rather than an individual phenomenon. Not coincidentally, a sense of mainstream national culture was just beginning to take shape at the time of Lind's US concert tour in the middle of the nineteenth century. She came to represent the ideal public musician in this period, not solely because of her personal musical accomplishments, but because of what newspapers wrote about her, how audiences reacted to her, and why people played and sang her repertoire for themselves.

As interesting as it is to study history and imagine living in a distant time with differing modes of transportation, communication, and engagement with music, one can also consider the legacy of Jenny Lind and her mid-nineteenth-century context in US popular music today. To be sure, much about the media for disseminating musical commodities has changed in the era of recorded sound and digitized production and marketing, but in considering the role of celebrity vis-à-vis mainstream musical culture today, we can find corollaries with history. With awareness of how cultural markers of gender, race, and class overlapped to construct Lind as an idealized public musician, we can better appreciate the role of these cultural markers in constructing musical celebrity today. For example, whose culture becomes "mainstream" and what identities are represented? What opposing qualities or pressures must today's artists bring into balance in order to experience popularity? How do audience expectations for representations of gender, class, and race shift, depending on musical genre or style? In this case, the study of what seems like the distant past may bring new understandings to the not-so-distant past.

THE MID-NINETEENTH CENTURY CONTEXT FOR POPULARITY AND CELEBRITY

The Swedish Nightingale came to epitomize US popular music success in part because of the timing of her mid-nineteenth-century tour. A sense of national mainstream culture was just then beginning to take shape, as people living in different regions of the nation shared more entertainment experiences. For example, new railroad lines allowed performers to travel more efficiently, while print media advertised and reviewed concerts for potential audiences nationwide who might greet the musicians later on their tours. In this era before recorded sound, most music heard on a daily basis was amateur music, played and sung in homes and communities for family and friends, and by the mid-nineteenth century, the growing music-publishing industry was distributing sheet music and books more quickly, providing shared access to the latest popular songs across different regions of the country. For the concept of "popular music" to have meaning, a mass audience needed to have access to shared musical experiences, and this was newly possible in the era of Lind's tour in the United States.

The concept of musical "celebrity" was also new in this period and required the interplay of efficient transportation and dissemination of print media. Aggressive marketing of the Swedish Nightingale contributed greatly to Lind's status as "superstar," to use the wording of Katherine Preston, a scholar of nineteenth-century opera in the United States.[6] Very early in the tour, newspapers were already proclaiming her popularity, unmatched by any contemporary singer: "The most popular woman in the world, at this moment—perhaps the most popular that ever was in it—is Jenny Lind. Other women have been favorites with a portion, and even a majority, of the public: she appears to be a favorite with all."[7] Newspapers across the country heightened anticipation for Lind's arrival in cities and towns across the Midwest and South by reporting on the overwhelmingly favorable audience reaction to her first concerts on the East Coast. Audience experience of attending her concerts was undoubtedly influenced by the advance praise printed widely in newspapers and magazines across the country. Needless to say, writing about Lind traveled farther than the live sound, and was thus hugely influential in shaping the Swedish Nightingale persona.

The success of Lind's US tour and indeed the spread of "Lind mania" had much to do with how audience expectations about gendered roles in society, racialized music performances, and musical taste as a marker of social class were discussed in contemporary periodical literature. Lind very quickly became a mainstream cultural icon, but she came to represent an idealized, upper-class, white femininity that was certainly not an identity or lifestyle shared by all Americans. Though the country included wealthy and powerful citizens, working-class immigrants, indentured servants, and enslaved Africans, the use of Lind to construct the mainstream image of idealized womanhood did not reflect this diversity. The Swedish Nightingale represented a version of femininity mostly associated with European Americans and middle- and upper-class access to leisure pursuits such as parlor music, concert attendance, and philanthropy.

Lind became a legendary popular-music success, and indeed a musical celebrity, because she also satisfied conflicting audience expectations. She displayed virtuosic professional musicianship, undoubtedly stemming from her rigorous training and previous operatic career, but did so in a seemingly "natural" way. She connected to audiences as an "authentic," "real" person with a humble stage presence while representing an idealized woman who exceeded the skill level and philanthropic activities of most American women. She sang performance repertoire that would have been familiar to amateur musicians in the audience as music they could sing themselves and combined this with numbers unique to her concerts. Operatic selections by Rossini and Donizetti common to the repertoire of touring opera stars facilitated display of cultivated *bel canto* technique (e.g., "Casta diva"[8]), while the singing of Swedish folk music (e.g., "Herdsman's Echo Song"),[9] US parlor music (e.g., "Home Sweet Home"),[10] and hymns helped her appear more ordinary. Balancing virtuosity and naturalness seemed to be a successful formula, and a closer look at the print media that framed Lind's concertizing reveals both virtuosity and naturalness to have interesting gender-, race-, and class-based connotations that overlapped to construct Lind as mainstream America's idealized vision of musical celebrity.

IDEALIZED GENDER ROLES AND RESPONSIBILITIES

Of these three social identity categories (gender, race, and class), gender is the one that scholars most often discuss in the context of Lind's popular success in the United States. This is because Lind entered the realm of public concert performance at a time when few middle-class women did. In the nineteenth century, the cult of "true womanhood" associated ideal femininity with domesticity, morality, passivity, and subservience. Virtuous womanhood was also associated with Christian religious images of angels and heaven.[11] The belief that society was divided into two spheres of influence, public and private, was widespread. Furthermore, the ideological linkage of masculinity with the public realm and femininity with the private was pervasive in the United States. In short, the ideal man worked out of the home, and the ideal woman worked in the home. Although women were widely expected to be musical amateurs in domestic spaces, women in public theater and musical performance were associated with low-class burlesque and even prostitution.[12] Lind's popularity seems in some ways to defy this conventional wisdom about nineteenth-century separate, gendered spheres of influence because her extensive public work did not tarnish her image as an ideal woman. She actually extended the ideals associated with pious femininity from the domestic to the public realm.[13]

As a woman representing middle-class domestic ideals, her presence on public concert stages may have been transgressive, but the repertoire she sang was acceptably feminine, in accordance with the social norms and tastes of her time. Sentimentality pervaded nineteenth-century cultural practices, especially literary and musical arts associated with women.[14] Female music making was "sentimental" when aiming to evoke prescribed emotional responses, especially surrounding nostalgia, love, and death. "Home Sweet Home" is an example of a sentimental song that was popular among amateurs and also a staple of Lind's performance repertoire.[15] Actually, much of Lind's repertoire would have been familiar to audience members because it circulated via sheet music for domestic amateur (especially female) performances. Some editions of the sheet music, including "Home Sweet Home," used Lind's name and portrait to help connect to and sell to female consumers. Concert reviews that describe effusive, emotional outpourings in reaction to Lind's singing voice are in keeping with the aesthetic of sentimental parlor songs.[16] Importantly, Lind's mid-century tour coincided with an increase in women in theater and concert audiences,[17] and by singing "their" music, she enabled middle- and upper-class women with access to parlor-music culture to have imaginary connections with Lind even without personally meeting her. Such connections lessened the impact of her transgression into the public sphere.

Lind connected to the growing number of women attending public theater and concert performances through her portrayal of authenticity balanced with idealized celebrity. This was especially important in the mid-nineteenth century, which some cultural historians have labeled an "age of cultural fraud," when many profitable entertainments (many organized and marketed by Lind's own manager, P. T. Barnum) took the form of dishonest masquerades designed to intrigue, if not trick, paying onlookers.[18] Unlike many other entertainments that Barnum marketed, Lind seemed real and sincere. Audiences were also accepting and sympathetic toward Lind because she displayed modesty and humility. For example, rather than feel threatened or intimidated by her public power to command huge audiences and make unprecedented sums of money, one St. Louis writer described Lind as timid and fragile on the concert stage.[19] Another described her "awkward step and school girl bow."[20] Contemporary writers linked her youthful, fragile femininity to genius. For example, "the slight, maidenly Jenny Lind" was said to have "mental superiority and the utmost delicacy of feeling, united to an originality of genius."[21] In these ways, her idealized feminine singing voice did not seem to threaten male dominance in the public sphere, as did women delivering public speeches in the same period.[22] Lind's performances were accepted as not only appropriately feminine but *ideally* feminine even though they were public.

Bird stage names for female singers were the norm for the period and reinforced the notion that women were supposed to be natural musicians. Lind toured as the Swedish Nightingale, contemporaneous with Catherine Hayes, the "Swan of Erin," and Elizabeth Taylor Greenfield, the "Black Swan." Many reviewers remarked that Lind's musicianship seemed natural and effortless, but even Lind's highly trained virtuosic vocal displays, which might have served to distance her from amateur musicians in the audience, actually served to further sentimental emotional outpourings.[23] For example, the popular women's magazine *Godey's Lady's Book* described "extreme delicacy" in her upper notes and the "bird-like ease with which she pours forth a flood of melody."[24] Her stage name worked in conjunction with the discourse of sentimentality to present Lind's voice and persona as pure and sweet—key elements of the femininity represented by Lind.

Perhaps most importantly, Lind's well-publicized charitable giving furthered the perception of her as an ideal woman. Even though her success was evidence of her competitive function in the entertainment business, people believed she did so in service of others, which was in keeping with nineteenth-century expectations for women to devote themselves to the spiritual, moral, and educational betterment of others. Furthermore, she chose politically neutral charitable causes such as widows, orphans, and schools, steering clear of controversy, and refusing to take a stand on slavery, for example, when many female philanthropists in the northern states were becoming abolitionists.[25] At a time when exaggerated self-denial, generosity, and philanthropy were expected of middle- and upper-class American women,[26] Lind's gifts to local charities were publicized from the beginning of her tour, as was her interest in keeping ticket prices low.[27] Both of these activities widened her appeal and lessened the appearance of her as inaccessible, elite, self-serving, or financially competitive.

Nineteenth-century American women were expected to be spiritual and moral compasses for men and children and religious leaders in homes. Thus, the extensive use of religious discourse to describe Lind's performance furthered her popularity and distanced her from morally suspect public performances. The *New York Herald* connected her idealized femininity to religiosity this way: "It is her high moral character—her spotless name, which the breath of slander has never tainted—her benevolence—her charity—her amiable temper—the religious sentiment which she so carefully cultivates."[28] The prominent US music critic who held great regard for the European concert music tradition, John Sullivan Dwight, wrote that "whether secular or sacred, music she sings naturally rises to the religious—leaves you stronger, calmer in your soul and not the victim of empty passion."[29] The "empty passion" here likely refers to lavish technical displays associated with some traveling instrumentalists and opera singers in the Romantic Era. Dwight also wrote that her singing was "like prayer" and "inspires deeper, holier feelings."[30] Here is how a writer for the *Ohio Statesman* described the religious influence of Lind's musical voice:

> Her work upon earth is a glorious and beneficent one. Heaven has endowed her with great power, and commissioned her to elevate the human heart, and fill it with happiness and love. She has been to the American people a ministering angel of joy. It must be a callous heart that will not ever remember that she has, while sojourning in this goodly land, been faithful and true to her heaven appointed mission.[31]

Periodicals also reported that her singing inspired good audience behavior.[32] Despite the large numbers of people assembled to greet her and attend her performances, news reports of disorder or disturbance are rare.

Through the lens of gender, we can see Lind as representing an idealized version of femininity. She connected to US audiences by representing skills and traits of some ordinary women and by exceeding them. In her public performances and philanthropy, she may have paved the way for other women to leave the private sphere for the stage, as some have argued,[33] but in representing leisure pursuits, values, and skills that were available primarily to upper social classes in the United States, she also perpetuated expectations that women in the public realm were supposed to be charitable—not pursuing popularity or personal profit as ends in themselves. The ideals of sentimental womanhood represented by the Swedish Nightingale cannot be understood in terms of gender alone because her version of femininity was so strongly shaped by middle- and upper-class values and pursuits that were inaccessible to the working women of the lower and middle classes who did not live a life of parlor music and philanthropy.

CLASS DISTINCTIONS AND CROSSINGS

Class differentiation was extremely important among nineteenth-century women on public stages. Lind's representation of idealized upper-class domestic values in the public realm ensured that she not be mistaken for a low-class burlesque performer or vilified as a prostitute.[34] Since the idealized femininity represented by Lind was not a lifestyle available to US women of all social classes, the connections she forged with audiences through common musical repertoire were strongest with those who had access to parlor culture, sheet music, pianos, and other instruments. In this context, Lind represented "correctness of taste" and "strength of judgment"[35] about European music, which had connotations of high culture. She also needed to avoid seeming elite, and her well-publicized involvement as bridesmaid at a servant's wedding helped US audiences think of her as approachable or even ordinary. Americans would have understood this participation in a lower-class woman's wedding as evidence of Lind's humility, modesty, and her devotion to serving others beneath her station.[36] This could have been interpreted not only as gendered behavior but also as a class crossing of sorts, when, for a brief ceremony, the celebrity stepped down to honor a servant. The appeal of this story involved its framing of Lind as unassuming and in touch with ordinary Americans. Lind attracted audiences of diverse social-class standing because she represented aspirational high culture without seeming elitist.

Lind's concerts facilitated acquisition of musical culture in between low and high class—a "middle class." Emerging class consciousness in mid-nineteenth-century America coincided with the idea that "middle class" was less of a defined subgroup in society and more of an aspirational ideal within reach of many or even all. "Middle class-ness," as one scholar termed it, was believed to be something that all could acquire through participation in public and domestic musical activities.[37] Musical luxuries traditionally affordable only to the upper classes were, in the nineteenth century, increasingly available to more Americans. By the mid-nineteenth century, the availability of less expensive factory-made upright pianos and mass distribution of published sheet music was widening participation in the types of social music making that once were associated with upper classes. Parlor music, pianos, and music literacy would still be out of reach for working-class Americans, such as the women who worked in factories and service jobs, but concert attendance could be an entry-level musical activity. Class consciousness, especially the new thinking about accessible middle class-ness, facilitated Lind's success and was encouraged by her US concertizing.

CULTURAL CONSTRUCTIONS OF RACE

The working-class women of the United States unrepresented by Lind's version of idealized, upper-class femininity were of various races and ethnic backgrounds, but Lind's rise to fame and the spread of her image of idealized femininity were a result of her outward appearance of whiteness and, more specifically, her Northern European origins. Periodical literature describes her physical appearance in overlapping gendered, classed, and racialized terms in order to differentiate her from other forms of contemporary popular music entertainment, including blackface minstrelsy and Italian opera. She's also set apart from the singer Elizabeth Taylor Greenfield, the African American singer whose first tour coincided with Lind's. Detailed mid-nineteenth-century descriptions of the physical appearance of stage performers might seem odd to today's readers. However, visual media was limited, and moreover,

Victorians believed in strong connections between morality and outward physical appearance.[38] Here is one of the descriptions that introduced Lind to New Yorkers:

> Jenny Lind has not a classical face, but, on the contrary, has a good deal both of the Scotch and northern German outline of features; while she possesses, at the same time, all of their sense, prudence, and high order of intellect. The southern Germans are more like the Italians—fiery, passionate, enthusiastic, and impulsive. These southern Europeans fall into errors from which the calculating caution of the northerners protects them. Jenny Lind has the enthusiasm of genius, but it is regulated by a cool judgment. It is not, then, for her beauty that she is so popular, though she possesses a fair share of personal attractions, and has a remarkably fine pair of blue eyes, revealing a bright intelligence within.[39]

Concepts linking facial features and eye color to moralized personality traits and intellectual capabilities were strongly tied to nineteenth-century theories about racial difference, which held that racial identity was not only physically apparent but also biologically determined and linked to predetermined personality and intellectual qualities. Thus, writing that emphasized Lind's "Nordic appearance" distinguished her from contemporary popular musical entertainments on the basis of race and, by extension, intellect and morality.[40]

Despite Lind's operatic training, prior experience performing opera in Europe, and her US concert programming that included many selections from Italian opera, writers in the musical press separated Lind from the field of Italian opera singers touring the United States in the mid-century period. John Sullivan Dwight, for example, was not a fan of Italian opera, which he called the "cheaper stimulus,"[41] compared with high praise for Lind's concerts. Drawing sharp distinction between her Northern European roots and the other singers who were Italian by birth and/

or training, writers referred to Lind's "Northern genius."[42] Dwight wrote that out of Sontag, Alboni, and Lind, Lind was the "only woman of actual genius" of the three and pointed also to her "natural gifts" and "positive genius."[43] The prevalence of the word *genius* is not incidental here, but used to communicate an assumption of ethnic/racial predetermination—not an accomplishment gained via education or training but supposedly one she was born into.

Although less famous than Lind, Greenfield actually toured the northern United States in exactly the same months as Lind, which enabled newspapers across the country to compare and contrast the two. Comparisons were strengthened by the facts that they sang similar repertoire, in many of the same concert halls, to presumably similar audiences. Many critics applauded Greenfield's accomplishments and apparent facility with a wide vocal range that exceeded Lind's. Newspapers that reviewed Greenfield's concerts conventionally contrasted the Black Swan, as Greenfield was known, with the Swedish Nightingale on the basis of race. Writers reserved the "genius" status for Lind and while acknowledging the power and facility in Greenfield's singing, they used her blackness to position her below Lind's celebrity status. Although there were many similarities in the concert programming and timing between these two vocalists, it is Lind who became mainstream America's vision of idealized celebrity, owing in large part to their different ethnic backgrounds and outward appearance.[44]

Marketing Lind's concerts as distinct from minstrel shows would seem like an easier task compared to navigating the field of contemporary singers whose concert repertoire overlapped so significantly with Lind's. Minstrelsy involved mostly white men with burnt cork makeup playing stock characters based on racist and sexist stereotypes. Minstrelsy was social and political comedy that ridiculed African Americans (both enslaved and free), women, and high culture. Needless to say, Jenny Lind's concerts were a far cry from the minstrel show and did not diminish the popularity of minstrelsy, which was a dominant form of popular music entertainment in northern cities through the Civil War period. However, while it drew mostly working-class white men in the early decades of its history (1830s–1840s), by mid-century, changes in programming toward the inclusion of more sentimental songs may have attracted more women. Thus, Barnum, in marketing Lind's concerts, was to some extent competing for the same audiences as minstrel companies. The constructions of Lind's idealized whiteness and genius did much to contrast her concerts with the minstrel shows understood at the time as presentations of low-class and "Black" music, even though few African Americans were involved in minstrel performances.

Lind's whiteness was used to align her more closely with orchestral music than these other forms of popular entertainment, thereby using race to bolster her heightened class standing. "Whiteness" was clearly a trait associated with her European heritage, and even more specifically, her Northern European ethnicity was valued. As printed in Lind's memoir, published to coincide with the US tour, "Of all the female vocalists that ever trod the lyrical stage, Jenny Lind may, more than any other, be entitled European."[45] Whiteness also aligned with feminine purity, and thus helped further perception of her idealized womanhood. It is useful to look at a given historical topic through multiple critical lenses (gender, class, race) in turn, but in so doing, one often sees how these identity markers overlap in significant ways. In this case, overlapping identity markers increased Lind's celebrity status and reinforced the notion that the norms for mainstream American popular music were not necessarily "normal" for all Americans.

Lind, performing as the Swedish Nightingale, ascended quickly to become mainstream America's most popular musical celebrity. Her timing was right, as necessary transportation and other elements of infrastructure that would enable the development of a nationwide music industry in the United States were coming together. At the time of Lind's tour, music and musicians could become "popular" in the United States more efficiently that in

earlier eras. Lind and her manager also had the cultural constructions right. Lind was appealing and attractive because she extended
idealized femininity of the domestic sphere to the public stage,
facilitated the middle-class acquisition of exclusive high culture,
and represented exclusive Northern European whiteness that had
cosmopolitan appeal. Lind's notoriety and tremendous popular
success as the Swedish Nightingale served to established norms
for mainstream American popular music that were not normal for
most Americans but replicated the types of gendered, class-based,
and racial identities of those holding power in US society.

I have focused this essay on the cultural making of Lind, the
Swedish Nightingale as she was known to audiences, partially to
provoke thought about similar musical-cultural relations today.
The United States is tremendously culturally diverse—even more
so today than during Lind's tour in the early 1850s. But when considering whose culture becomes mainstream today, is the diversity
of the audience represented? Lind's tremendous popularity cannot
be explained simply by pointing to what must have been an attractive singing voice; likewise, the success of today's stars cannot be
attributed to their voice alone. In fact, even though the recorded
and digitally manipulated sound of popular singers is ubiquitous
in US culture today, it would be easy to argue that the sound of
the most popular stars is inseparable from visual images, especially
since the 1980s and the advent of the music video. The US and
global music industry today is more complex compared with that
which existed before the recorded-sound era, in part because of
the proliferation of styles and genres that serve as marketing categories. When considering what opposing qualities or pressures
today's artists must bring into balance in order to experience popularity, the answer is different depending on the style/genre and
perceived demographics of the target market. Interestingly, that
target market and the perception of shared identity factors (such as
gender, class, and race) may be strengthened by the music marketing, not merely stemming in one direction from culture. Needless

to say, popular music is as difficult to disentangle from culture today as it was in the nineteenth century.

NOTES

1. Gladys Denny Shultz, *Jenny Lind, The Swedish Nightingale* (Philadelphia and New York: Lippincott, 1962), 177–79.
2. Porter W. Ware and Thaddeus Constantine Lockard, *P. T. Barnum Presents Jenny Lind: The American Tour of the Swedish Nightingale* (Baton Rouge: Louisiana State University Press, 1980), 45; *Washington Daily National Intelligencer* Washington, DC, December 4, 1850.
3. Shultz, *Jenny Lind*, 190.
4. *Scioto Gazette* (Chillicothe, OH), July 26, 1850; *Raleigh Register* (Raleigh, NC), July 27, 1850; *Cleveland Herald* (Cleveland, Ohio), August 1, 1850; *Raleigh Register* (Raleigh, NC), August 3, 1850; *Daily National Intelligencer* (Washington, DC), August 1, 1850; *Boston Daily Atlas* (Boston, MA), August 7, 1850.
5. Shultz, *Jenny Lind*.
6. Katherine K. Preston, *Opera on the Road: Traveling Opera Troupes in the United States, 1825–60* (Urbana: University of Illinois Press, 1993), 153.
7. *New York Herald*, September 6, 1850.
8. *Bel canto* means "beautiful singing" in Italian and is a term used to describe the high, light, sometimes heavily ornamented singing style common in the professional performance of nineteenth-century Italian opera. See V. Bellini, "Casta diva = Virgin spirit," cavatina [from] the opera *Norma* (New York: Wm. Vanderbeek, 1851), https://www.loc.gov/item/sm1851.490460/.
9. Maurice Strakosck, "Herdsman's Echo Song," *Music Copyright Deposits, 1820–1860* (New York: William Hall and Son, 1850
10. Samuel Owen, "Jenny Lind's 'Home Sweet Home,'" *Music Copyright Deposits, 1820–1860* (New York: Firth, Pond, 1851).
11. Barbara Welter, "The Cult of True Womanhood: 1820-1860," *American Quarterly* 18, no. 2, part 1 (Summer 1966): 152–53.
12. Robert G. Allen, *Horrible Prettiness: Burlesque and American Culture* (Chapel Hill: University of North Carolina Press, 1991), 51–52.
13. For further discussion about nineteenth-century middle-class women exerting influence despite having little tangible power, see Ann Douglas, *The Feminization of American Culture* (New York: Farrar, Strauss & Giroux, 1998), 8–9.
14. Shirley Samuels, introduction to *The Culture of Sentiment: Race, Gender, and Sentimentality in 19th Century America*, ed. Shirley Samuels (New York: Oxford

University Press, 1992), 4. Relatedly, music making featured prominently in sentimental novels to portray idealized nineteenth-century women, according to Petra Meyer-Frazier, "Music, Novels, and Women: Nineteenth-Century Prescriptions for an Ideal Life," *Women and Music* 10 (2006): 45–59.

15. Shultz, *Jenny Lind*, 246.
16. G. G. Foster, ed., *Memoir of Jenny Lind* (New York: Dewitt & Davenport, 1850), 3.
17. Allen, *Horrible Prettiness*, 70.
18. James W. Cook, *The Arts of Deception: Playing with Fraud in the Age of Barnum* (Cambridge, MA: Harvard University Press, 2001), 1–11.
19. Quoted in Ware and Lockard, *P. T. Barnum Presents Jenny Lind*, 24.
20. *Cleveland Herald* (Cleveland, Ohio), November 8, 1851.
21. Foster, *Memoir*, 4.
22. Roberta Montemorra Marvin, "Idealizing the *Prima Donna* in Mid-Victorian London," in *The Arts of the Prima Donna in the Long Nineteenth Century,* ed. Rachel Cowgill and Hilary Poriss (New York: Oxford University Press, 2012), 24.
23. Rebeccah Bechtold, "'She Sings a Stamp of Originality': Sentimental Mimicry in Jenny Lind's American Tour," *ESQ: A Journal of the American Renaissance* 58, no. 4 (2012): 497.
24. "Editors' Table," *Godey's Lady's Book*, vol. 42, February 1851, 134–35.
25. Brian Roberts, *Blackface Nation: Race, Reform, and Identity in American Popular Music, 1812–1925* (Chicago: University of Chicago Press, 2017), 212.
26. Hilary Poriss, "Prima Donnas and the Performance of Altruism," in *The Arts of the Prima Donna in the Long Nineteenth Century,* ed. Rachel Cowgill and Hilary Poriss (New York: Oxford University Press, 2012), 44.
27. Ware and Lockard, *P. T. Barnum Presents Jenny Lind*, 44; *Boston Daily Atlas* (Boston, MA) November 27, 1851; Shultz, *Jenny Lind*, 228.
28. *New York Herald*, September 6, 1850.
29. *Dwight's Journal of Music*, May 15, 1852, 42.
30. *Dwight's Journal of Music*, May 22, 1852, 53.
31. *Daily Ohio Statesman* (Columbus, OH) November 6, 1851.
32. Gustavus Stadler, "Cosmopolitan Whiteness: Writing Jenny Lind," in *Troubling Minds: The Cultural Politics of Genius in the United States, 1840-1890* (Minneapolis: University of Minnesota Press, 2006), 57–59.
33. Adrienne Fried Block, "Two Virtuoso Performers in Boston: Jenny Lind and Camilla Urso," in *New Perspectives on Music: Essays in Honor of Eileen Southern,* ed. Josephine Wright and Samuel A. Floyd (Warren, MI: Harmonie Park Press, 1992), 371.

34. Maria-Elena Buszek, "Representing 'Awarishness': Burlesque, Feminist Transgression, and the 19th-Century Pin-up," *TDR* 43, no. 4 (Winter 1999): 141.
35. Ware and Lockard, *P. T. Barnum Presents Jenny Lind*, 28.
36. Ware and Lockard, *P. T. Barnum Presents Jenny Lind*, 111.
37. Daniel Cavicchi, *Listening and Longing: Music Lovers in the Age of Barnum* (Middletown, CT: Wesleyan University Press, 2011), 26.
38. Marvin, "Idealizing the *Prima Donna*," 28.
39. *New York Herald*, September 6, 1850.
40. Stadler, "Cosmopolitan Whiteness," 36.
41. *Dwight's Journal of Music*, 42.
42. *Dwight's Journal of Music*, 41.
43. *Dwight's Journal of Music*, December 4, 1852, 67.
44. Julia J. Chybowski, "Becoming the 'Black Swan' in Mid-Nineteenth-Century America: Elizabeth Taylor Greenfield's Early Life and Debut Concert Tour," *Journal of the American Musicological Society* 67, no. 1 (Spring 2014): 125–65.
45. Foster, *Memoir of Jenny Lind*, 3.

SELECTED BIBLIOGRAPHY

Scholarly Books and Articles

Allen, Robert G. *Horrible Prettiness: Burlesque and American Culture*. Chapel Hill: University of North Carolina Press, 1991.

Bechtold, Rebeccah. "'She Sings a Stamp of Originality': Sentimental Mimicry in Jenny Lind's American Tour." *ESQ: A Journal of the American Renaissance* 58, no. 4 (2012): 493–528.

Block, Adrienne Fried. "Two Virtuoso Performers in Boston: Jenny Lind and Camilla Urso." In *New Perspectives on Music: Essays in Honor of Eileen Southern*, edited by Josephine Wright and Samuel A. Floyd. Warren, MI: Harmonie Park Press, 1992.

Buszek, Maria-Elena. "Representing 'Awarishness': Burlesque, Feminist Transgression, and the 19th-Century Pin-up." *TDR* 43, no. 4 (Winter 1999): 141–62.

Cavicchi, Daniel. *Listening and Longing: Music Lovers in the Age of Barnum*. Middletown, CT: Wesleyan University Press, 2011.

Chybowski, Julia J. "Becoming the 'Black Swan' in Mid-Nineteenth-Century America: Elizabeth Taylor Greenfield's Early Life and Debut Concert Tour." *Journal of the American Musicological Society* 67, no. 1 (Spring 2014): 125–65.

Cook, James W. *The Arts of Deception: Playing with Fraud in the Age of Barnum*. Cambridge, MA: Harvard University Press, 2001.

Douglas, Ann. *The Feminization of American Culture*. New York: Farrar, Strauss & Giroux, 1998.

Foster, G. G., ed. *Memoir of Jenny Lind*. New York: Dewitt & Davenport, 1850.

Marvin, Roberta Montemorra. "Idealizing the Prima Donna in Mid-Victorian London." In *The Arts of the Prima Donna in the Long Nineteenth Century*, edited by Rachel Cowgill and Hilary Poriss. New York: Oxford University Press, 2012.

Meyer-Frazier, Petra. "Music, Novels, and Women: Nineteenth-Century Prescriptions for an Ideal Life." *Women and Music* 10 (2006): 45–59.

Poriss, Hilary. "Prima Donnas and the Performance of Altruism." In *The Arts of the Prima Donna in the Long Nineteenth Century*, edited by Rachel Cowgill and Hilary Poriss. New York: Oxford University Press, 2012.

Preston, Katherine K. *Opera on the Road: Traveling Opera Troupes in the United States, 1825–60*. Urbana: University of Illinois Press, 1993.

Roberts, Brian. *Blackface Nation: Race, Reform, and Identity in American Popular Music, 1812–1925*. Chicago: University of Chicago Press, 2017.

Samuels, Shirley, ed. *The Cultural Sentiment: Race, Gender, and Sentimentality in 19th Century America*. New York: Oxford University Press, 1992.

Shultz, Gladys Denny. *Jenny Lind, The Swedish Nightingale*. Philadelphia and New York: Lippincott, 1962.

Stadler, Gustavus. *Troubling Minds: The Cultural Politics of Genius in the United States, 1840–1890*. Minneapolis: University of Minnesota Press, 2006.

Ware, Porter, and Thaddeus Constantine Lockard. *P. T. Barnum Presents Jenny Lind: The American Tour of the Swedish Nightingale*. Baton Rouge: Louisiana State University Press, 1980.

Welter, Barbara. "The Cult of True Womanhood: 1820–1860." *American Quarterly* 18, no. 2, part 1 (Summer 1966): 151–74.

Nineteenth-Century Periodicals

Boston Daily Atlas (Boston, MA), August 7 and November 27, 1850.

Cleveland Herald (Cleveland, OH), August 1 and November 8, 1851.

Daily Ohio Statesman (Columbus, OH) November 6, 1851.

Daily National Intelligencer (Washington, DC), August 1 and December 4 1850.

Dwight's Journal of Music, May 15, May 22, December 4, 1852.

Godey's Lady's Book, vol. 42, February 1851, 134–35.

New York Herald, September 6, 1850.

Raleigh Register (Raleigh, NC), July 27 and August 3, 1850.

Scioto Gazette (Chillicothe, OH), July 26, 1850.

LISTENING TO MUSIC HISTORY

Nathan C. Bakkum

INTRODUCTION

I am a musicologist, a bassist, a songwriter, and a creative musician. I engage with the world first and foremost through sound, and I understand time—the flow of a workday, the pacing of a project, the changing of the seasons—in musical terms. Music is my way of being in the world, and it structures my interactions with family, friends, colleagues, students, and strangers.

Before I earned any academic credential in music, I studied to be a teacher. I recognize that the choices we make about the content, structure, and experiences that organize our classrooms inevitably amplify certain perspectives, identities, and experiences while silencing others. In my work as a scholar and educator, I have tried to undo some of the more persistent assumptions that animate most music history courses, and I have tried to build systems and experiences that honor the wide variety of backgrounds and goals that students bring to the classroom. At the same time, I have focused on exploring musical histories and cultures through methods and models that resonate with the various ways that musicians participating in different traditions practice their craft. In all of this, I have foregrounded questions of historiography, asking students to consider the choices made by historians and musicians as they construct musical and historical narratives while also inviting students to participate in history making of their own.

My primary research has focused on musical and social interaction between improvising musicians in jazz ensembles and the ways that those interactions are mediated by recordings. From that foundation, I have explored the particular historical and interactive logics of hip-hop musicians, the complex aesthetic and economic interplay that drives the production of much US popular music, and the fundamental distortions that are required in order to engage such traditions in the context of modern collegiate music programs. What kinds of stories best illuminate the world and work of a producer like J Dilla? What kind of education would support and prepare the next Kendrick Lamar? In this essay, I attempt to pull together many of these threads into a consideration of relationships among teachers, students, musical practices, recordings, and history.

This is a story about how we tell stories and how some of those stories reflect how recordings are made and how they circulate. Such stories help us make sense of our daily experience, and they help us explain who we are and where we came from. We use storytelling to create the very world around us and to locate ourselves in relation to one another. Like so many other stories, this one is about repetition and change. It's also a story about paying attention to the glorious details embedded in records.

Less than one hundred and fifty years ago, the experience of music was an exclusively physical and social one; hearing new works or old favorites required the listener to witness—or participate in—a performance as it happened. Today, listeners have ready access to millions of pieces of music, and recordings soundtrack every moment of our days. Each listener encounters the music's history along their own personal path—discovering new artists, styles, and innovations asynchronously and at varying depths. Mozart, Madonna, and the Modern Jazz Quartet happily coexist— just a short scroll or a quick search separating them in our music libraries. We might meet these artists in any order, building a personal musical history that is unique to us. And yet, this endless musical landscape has been curated for generations. The stories that scholars, journalists, friends, and relatives tell about music can often shape our experience just as deeply and meaningfully as the sounds themselves. Those stories are far from neutral, as individuals have chosen to privilege particular types of music making, particular types of musicians, and particular stories that weave together a history that resonates in a specific way or for a specific group of people. For every story we tell, we leave dozens untold.

How has sound recording changed the way that we engage with and make sense of this world of music? How has it changed our role as listeners and explorers? How might we begin to construct new stories that allow us to make sense of all of the voices swirling through our headphones? This essay engages with all of these questions by pulling together ideas from a broad range of thinkers and makers—including scholars and writers, composers and performers, recordists and listeners—who have focused their attention on how we experience recorded sound. Though it only scratches the surface of these questions, this essay outlines some of the ways that our approaches to listening are affected by recordings, and it points toward some ways in which many of our assumptions about history are out of step with our experience as listeners. Ultimately, I hope that this work invites readers to participate in the creation of personal and collective historical narratives that are more flexible, inclusive, and responsive to the daily work of musicians

SPIN THE BLACK CIRCLE: LISTENING AND REPETITION[1]

I listen with the assumption of repetition. When hearing a new piece of music for the first time, I often anticipate the opportunity to revisit tracks and moments that excite, move, or bewilder me. Asked my opinions on new music, I may remark that I "need to spend more time" with a particularly dense or meaningful album. Gradually, I take ownership of certain recordings, anticipating favorite musical ideas and transforming myself from a passive outsider to an active participant in the music. Even before recordings were invented, taking ownership of a piece of music required a similarly gradual process. For example, an amateur pianist in the nineteenth century would slowly gain intimacy with new repertoire through practice and repetition, feeling the music in his or her body as he or she develops an understanding of the contours and forms through performance. Today, we can similarly embody the content of recordings by singing along, playing air guitar, dancing, nodding, or just listening closely.[2]

Theorists and critics have concerned themselves with the effects of recording on listeners for nearly the entire expanse of the recorded age. In his 1938 essay "On the Fetish-Character in Music and the Regression of Listening," Theodor Adorno decries the twin evils of popular music and the economic system that supports it.[3] He argues that recordings fundamentally change the relationship between music and listener, replacing a focus on deep, personal experience with a compulsion to own and control musical objects.[4] In this new relationship, listeners are absolved of their responsibility to listen actively and participate in the process of interpreting the sounds they hear. Instead, Adorno says of popular music, "To like it is almost the same thing as to recognize it."[5] Rather than guiding listeners to draw connections between sections of a piece, recognizing how themes transform and forms unfold, Adorno argues that popular songs reward listeners for recognizing small-scale variations and momentary surprises within simple, repetitious forms. The twelve-bar blues moves relentlessly through its repeating harmonic progression. No matter the musical choices made by Louis Armstrong, Buddy Guy, or Etta Baker, none of these musicians disrupts the steady twelve-measure cycle at the form's core. This, for Adorno, is the great failing of popular music and the recorded music of the 1930s: the repetition of the record itself is reinforced by a repeating musical structure, both of which serve to pacify listeners and short circuit the dialogue between composer and audience. Of course, there is a racial dynamic at play here as well. Adorno champions upper-class European models of musical structure and complexity while disparaging the cyclical forms and variation processes associated with music of the African diaspora. By claiming the superiority of European musical aesthetics, he also asserts the superiority of European composers, performers, and audiences.

In a slightly more generous essay from the same era, Walter Benjamin agrees that something essential is certainly lost in the process of turning an artistic performance into a mass-produced product. In his 1936 piece "The Work of Art in the Age of Mechanical Reproduction," Benjamin argues that the fundamental spirit of an artwork cannot be reproduced. He writes, "Even the most perfect reproduction of a work of art is lacking in one element: its presence in time and space, its unique existence at the place where it happens to be."[6] In Benjamin's eyes, all reproductions are imperfect photocopies: they capture the outlines of the original, but the artwork's magical core essence escapes. He calls this ineffable spirit "aura" and argues that the work of art in the age of mechanical reproduction is the work of art without aura. In the end, however, Benjamin praises the broad accessibility of mass-mediated art, suggesting that film and recorded music might significantly elevate and educate a broad audience. But this expansion is not without a cost.

When Adorno and Benjamin published these ideas in the 1930s, the central place of recordings within broader understandings of musical aesthetics, economies, and social relations was not yet fully established. While these authors paid close attention to the experience of audiences as they engaged with recorded media, sound recordings also served to connect listeners to extramusical experiences in new ways. William Howland Kenney demonstrates that these connections date to the earliest days of sound recording.[7] In his book *Recorded Music in American Life: The Phonograph and Popular Memory, 1890–1945*, Kenney analyzes a broad cross section of responses to a 1921 survey of listeners conducted by Thomas A. Edison, Inc., the makers of one of the first commercially successful phonographs. In their responses, many listeners' appreciation for the phonographs in their homes was intimately tied to feelings of nostalgia and important personal memories. Respondents reported that certain songs transported them to other times and other locations, connecting them with family and friends who were lost or distant. Through their "phonographic remembering," listeners could take control of their past as they "repeatedly summoned forth the music that stimulated the emotions linked to memory."[8] This visceral experience of the past through a specific sonic anchor has become an essential use of recorded music, one that binds us together while fracturing the idea of a unitary, definitive story of history.

We are now nearly a century into an era in which many of us listen to music primarily (or exclusively) through mediated means. In this activity, we have executed a shift in the ways that we perceive the relationship between live and recorded sounds. We judge live performances against recorded archetypes, expecting fidelity to an imaginary standard constructed in the recording studio. As Greg Milner writes,

> What's contained on the record is not a document of a real-time event because there never *was* a real-time event. An average radio pop song may have the structure of a self-contained performance, of musicians playing off one another, but there is a good chance that none of these musicians were ever in the same room at the same time—if the record contains samples, the musicians may be separated by *decades*—so what event, exactly, is the record recording?[9]

As listeners, we have normalized this intense collaborative construction process as "the way music sounds," sometimes struggling in our appreciation of in-person musical performances that fail to meet this hyperreal, hyper-curated standard. H. Stith Bennett coined the phrase "recording consciousness" to describe this uniquely modern expectation.[10] In his consideration of the phenomenon, Richard Middleton writes, "This consciousness defines the social reality of popular music, and live performances have to try to approximate the sounds which inhabit this consciousness. Even when they fail, or it is impracticable, an audience's collective memory takes over and it 'hears' what it cannot hear, in the 'sketch' provided by the band."[11] We have come to hear the calculated construction of recordings as natural representations of performance, and in some cases, the experience of being in a room together and participating in music-making experiences has suffered because it fails to live up to our collective memory of those idealized performances.

MY BACK PAGES: RECORDING AND CHRONOLOGY[12]

Recordings are not music. Not precisely, anyway. Recordings are a medium of capture, construction, and communication—they are artifacts that document and demonstrate a particular kind of work that is done by musicians. This work—the daily practice undertaken by composers, performers, and recordists—is the real substance of this thing we call *music*. Christopher Small writes, "Music is not a thing at all but an activity, something people do. The apparent thing 'music' is a figment, an abstraction of the action, whose reality vanishes as soon as we examine it at all closely."[13] Recordings provide music with a particularly sticky form of thingness; LPs and CDs require physical space and specialized playback equipment. Even MP3s and other digital formats take up storage space or streaming bandwidth. It's easy to project all of our subtle, personal definitions of music onto those objects and forget that recordings are a medium through which we can actively engage with a wide world of musicians, sounds, and ideas. And yet, recordings have become the central artifact for students and scholars of modern music, providing essential evidence about what it means to be a musician in different times and spaces.

Recordings can trick us into thinking we have the whole picture. We hear the Rev. Dr. Martin Luther King Jr. proclaim the words "I have a dream"[14] and we are transported to the steps of the Lincoln Memorial in 1963. We feel the energy of the crowd and the passion of Dr. King, and we become participants in this historic moment. But the capture is always incomplete. We cannot hear how the amplified sound of his voice reverberated through the National Mall. We cannot hear the chants of supporters or protestors. We cannot imagine what it would have sounded like to stand next to Dr. King and hear his unamplified voice. We hear a partial, selective capture of the moment, and we fill in the rest with the help of our recording consciousness.

The incomplete nature of recordings isn't limited to the details of how they are produced. As listeners, we all discover particular recordings at different times and in different orders based on our own access, experiences, preferences, and social situations. This has always been the case; the invention of recordings just made this nonlinearity much more obvious. In my own experience as an orchestral bassist, I fell in love with Ludwig van Beethoven (1770–1827) and Samuel Barber (1910–1981) before I really discovered Johann Sebastian Bach (1685–1750), and my most powerful early encounters with Bach were through the twentieth-century orchestrations made by such conductors as Leopold Stokowski and Eugene Ormandy. My path was influenced by the choices of my teachers and conductors, but perhaps the biggest factor was simply the fact that I played the bass and therefore was exposed to music written for bassists.

While I might hear D'Angelo's *Black Messiah* (2014) as a return to the politically engaged soul and funk of 1970s-era Marvin Gaye and

George Clinton, another listener might only discover Parliament Funkadelic's *Chocolate City* after falling in love with D'Angelo's "The Charade." In that case, which came first? While we can empirically confirm that *Chocolate City* was released thirty-nine years earlier than *Black Messiah*, the relationship between these albums is inherently personal and tied to the experience of individual listeners and the musicians involved in their production. Of course, this interplay between musicians and audiences has always been at the core of musical practice. Performers have always intervened between composers and listeners, turning musical texts into sound through the imaginative deployment of refined technique. Yet, our stories have continued to foreground the technical innovations of composers while downplaying the influence of performers, audiences, and countless other participants in the collaborative making of musical meaning.[15]

At this point, you might ask whether recordings simply replace scores at the heart of our historical narratives. While we can never fully displace the materiality of recordings, these recorded "texts" are considerably more multivocal, shareable, and participatory than scores. Through recordings, we experience music history not as a memory or as a secondhand story; we encounter history as an active experience of musicking. In this process, the "there and then" of history—the conditions, expectations, and imaginations of composers, performers, and listeners from another time and place—is automatically and inextricably linked to the here and now of our listening in the present day. When we listen, we might be transported to another time and place as we develop an empathetic connection with a composer or performer. But that connection always forms in the present, filtered through the sea of media, information, and experience that define our modern landscape. Recordings push us to participate in the making of musical and historical meaning.

When we participate, we create. We put together ideas in novel and surprising ways. We make connections between parts of our personal experience and parts of the art and the history that we study. When we participate, we disagree. We see things others cannot, and we encounter blind spots that we didn't know we had. When we participate, we imagine. We fill in the blanks between data points and reconstruct sounds that were never played. Together, we build music history into a messy, confused, rich, and uncertain terrain that could never be captured in a textbook. When we participate in the construction of our own history—as recordings force us to do—music history becomes a living thing that we can manipulate, fight about, create, demolish, and recreate as it suits us. We become makers and destroyers of worlds.

Because so many modern musical styles have been comprehensively recorded and distributed as sonic objects, it's easy to assume that recordings tell the complete story. As Jed Rasula writes, "The act of writing a history must covertly contend with a history already in the process of transcribing itself, rendering the historian's account a surrogate act masquerading as authority."[16] Recordings create a loop in the history-making process, providing a type of evidence-as-experience, a much thicker and more comprehensive account of a moment than could possibly be captured through written or spoken means. Nonetheless, recordings—and historical narratives—are never neutral. They always represent a particular perspective, informed by the interests and experience of the people making the recording, the limitations of available technology, and the circumstances of a specific moment.

FIGHT THE POWER: RECORDING AND SILENCE[17]

With great power comes great responsibility. For every story captured or constructed through recording, thousands are left untold. Access to tens of millions of tracks on streaming services does not guarantee a level playing field. Certain recordings—and the mythologies that surround them—have solidified into stories that have been repeated forcefully enough that they have taken on the authority of fact. These stories crowd out alternatives that explore the same traditions through other people's eyes and ears. Elijah Wald makes this point in his provocatively titled book *How the Beatles Destroyed Rock 'n' Roll*.[18] In the book, Wald offers a history of American popular music written around the music that was most popular in its moment, rather than focusing solely on the music that seems most significant in retrospect. He writes,

> The critic's job is to assign value and importance on an artistic level, which necessarily is a judgment about how the work stands up in the present. The historian's is to sort out and explain what happened in the past, which means attempting to understand the tastes and environment of an earlier time. And the latter task also involves sorting out and understanding how earlier critics and historians were affected by their own times.[19]

Some historians would quibble with Wald's brief job description, but all would agree that we inherit a set of deeply embedded assumptions from earlier generations that inform the choices that we make about which pieces of music we value, which styles and ideas attract our attention, and which assumptions form the foundation of the stories we choose to tell. Chief among these assumptions is the idea that history progresses in an orderly and linear fashion that can be captured in a clear narrative and packaged in a textbook or a course syllabus. Hopefully, the previous sections of this essay have succeeded in challenging that idea.

Michel-Rolph Trouillot lays out the stakes of this particular assumption in his book *Silencing the Past: Power and the Production of History*.[20] Trouillot amplifies the aphorism that "history is written by the victors," arguing that historical narratives have consistently succeeded in erasing the stories of countless people, movements, and nations through the history-making process. Specifically, he draws our attention to four moments when silences are introduced in the time between when an event happens (e.g.,

Elvis Presley first learns Arthur Crudup's song "That's All Right, Mama"[21]) and when we write about it as history (e.g., some critics tout Presley's 1954 recording as the first rock 'n' roll record).[22] Trouillot writes, "Silences enter that process of historical production at four crucial moments: the moment of fact creation (the making of *sources*); the moment of fact assembly (the making of *archives*); the moment of fact retrieval (the making of *narratives*); and the moment of retrospective significance (the making of *history* in the final instance)."[23] In other words, historians make a lot of choices about who to trust, whose choices are significant, what materials are worth saving, and how those materials fit together to tell the stories that we call history. More often than not, those choices have been made in ways that privilege the experiences of dominant groups—Anglo-American, male, heterosexual, wealthy—while sidelining those who do not fit the bill. These layers of power are at the very root of the idea that Elvis's recording of "That's All Right" should be marked as the first rock 'n' roll record at all, as opposed to recordings by Jackie Brentson or Big Mama Thornton that also demonstrate many hallmarks of the style. In a world full of musicians expressing incredibly diverse perspectives and reflecting an equally diverse range of backgrounds, the kinds of silences that have supported the construction of music history do not reflect our musical reality.

That said, the white, upper-class, heteronormative archetypes that underpin the most commonly told stories about art music are embedded quite deeply in the ways that we think and talk about other styles and traditions. In the most general terms, the story goes like this: A young creative musician learns the foundations of the craft from an established master. He (it's almost always a he) pushes tirelessly against the walls of tradition, eventually birthing a technical breakthrough that leads to new ways of writing or playing music. In his time, some conservative musicians reject this innovation. In retrospect, we are able to look back and see the profound importance and broad influence of this restless genius.

This is the rough outline of the story that we tell about Bee-thoven and Igor Stravinsky.[24] It is also the story that we have come to tell about Sarah Vaughan and Miles Davis, the Beatles and Nirvana, Grandmaster Flash and Missy Elliott. But Vaughan and Davis were members of ensembles first and foremost; they consistently surrounded themselves with talented and inventive collaborators who would challenge them and introduce new ideas. The Beatles had George Martin and the vast resources of EMI Records at their disposal. Elliott worked with teams of producers, lyricists, and publicists in pursuing her craft as a songwriter, singer, and MC. It's impossible to suggest that all of these stories followed the same trajectory and relied on the same notions of musical individuality and authorship. Simply put, musicians emerging from different traditions and making music for different functions will inevitably pull the past together in different ways to tell their own story in the present.

Then why do we assume that all of music history moves in the same straight line? Johann Kroier asserts that this is a reflection of Western colonial power:

The relationship between European dominance in an imperial sense and the dominance of European music is not a causal one, nor one of direct mirroring. On the European side it is mediated by scientific, technological, and political dominance, while music itself is justified by theoretical, historical, and aesthetic discourses. Nevertheless, on the part of the colonial subject European dominance is experienced in a holistic way: in the form of institutions, prohibitions, coercion, education, moral admonition, and racist disdain.[25]

In other words, the assumptions that we make about how history works, what should be prized, and what should be ignored are products of a violent history that has long taught us that some people are valued and others are not. The ubiquity of recordings—and the messy, confused, ambiguous histories that they offer—challenges us to think about other ways of assessing value and constructing alternative narratives.

SEPARATE WAYS: ALTERNATIVES[26]

In the film based on Nick Hornby's novel *High Fidelity*, John Cusack plays Rob Gordon, a Chicago-based record store owner with vast knowledge of popular music recordings and a massive personal collection of vinyl albums. After going through a difficult breakup with his longtime girlfriend, Rob takes solace in the only place that offers him true comfort: his record collection. At a key scene in the film,[27] Rob's employee, Dick, comes to Rob's apartment to check on him, only to find stacks of vinyl piled throughout the living space. Dick knowingly assesses the situation, acknowledges that Rob is reorganizing his record collection, and asks him what system he is using. "Chronological?" Dick asks. "Not alphabetical," he continues. Dick gasps when Rob replies, "Autobiographical." Rob continues, "I can tell you how I got from Deep Purple to Howlin' Wolf in just twenty-five moves. And if I want to find the song 'Landslide' by Fleetwood Mac, I have to remember that I bought it for someone in the 'fall of 1983' pile but didn't give it to them for personal reasons."[28]

Rob finds his own identity in the midst of his personal sonic history, and his story is as real as any other. Even a stereotypically arrogant record store owner can make no claim of ultimate authority; the world of music, recordings, and information is simply too vast for any individual narrative to encompass all of it. The most honest, direct way that we can engage with music history is as we encounter it—personally, intimately, socially, and gradually. Individual personal histories form an essential foundation for thinking about music history, and such personal histories deeply inform the choices made by musicians and listeners. In many circumstances, a moment of musical autobiography provides the key to unlocking a wealth of personal and shared stories and ideas, revealing shifts and changes for musicians and audiences alike.

Sometimes these stories can be too restless and too fanciful—too personal—to be useful in communicating our historical insight to others. But what are some other models that might allow us to develop shared ways of conceptualizing music history without relying on master narratives and linear development? What follows are a few ideas that I have used to frame musical stories with my students. Each of these models relies in some way on the influence of recordings—as sonic materials to be manipulated, as a springboard toward inspiration or technical study, or as a commercial product that supports an industry. Each model also draws us as listeners into the history-making process, asking us to use recordings as a tool to make connections across time and space. These are just a few such ideas; you're welcome to imagine your own.

A Sedimentary History: Hip-Hop

Sample-based hip-hop presents a series of vexing questions about how we construct both music and history. A Kanye West track[29] based on a 1965 Nina Simone recording[30] most certainly qualifies as *new*. At the same time, the track draws depth and context from its association with the sampled source. The music's groove, harmonic structure, and formal shape emerge from several generations of interactions—Simone's interpretive relationship to the song, the relationships between Simone and the musicians and recording personnel involved in her 1965 recording, and the relationship between Simone's recording and the layers of music added by West and his team of producers. A full historical accounting of the song—and of sample-based hip-hop in general—requires us to consider multiple timelines, multiple contexts, and the active process through which hip-hop producers go about constructing these relationships. Joseph Schloss offers an extended look at this process in action:

Today, the term "break" refers to *any* segment of music (usually four measures or less) that could be sampled and repeated. For example, the song "They Reminisce Over You (T.R.O.Y.)," by Pete Rock and C. L. Smooth (1992) is based on a break from a late-sixties jazz artist. The break in this case, however, is not a moment of intense drum activity but a two-measure excerpt from a saxophone solo. Presumably one who was not already familiar with the hip-hop song would not hear those particular measures as being significant in the context of the original music. In contemporary terms, then, a break is any expanse of music that is *thought of as a break* by a producer. On a conceptual level, this means that the break in the original jazz record was brought into existence retroactively by Pete Rock's use of it. In other words, for the twenty-four years between its release and the day Pete Rock sampled it, the original song contained no break. From that day on, it contained the break from "They Reminisce Over You." Producers deal with this apparent breaching of the time-space continuum with typically philosophical detachment. Conventionally, they take the position that the break had always been there; it just took a great producer to hear and exploit it. Record collecting is approached as if potential breaks have been unlooped and hidden randomly throughout the world's music. It is the producer's job to find them.[31]

Hip-hop producers are musical archaeologists, literally digging through the vast scope of recorded music history, unearthing forgotten stories, and piecing together new narratives that resonate in our modern ears. In the process, they inevitably change the ways that we hear and understand their sampled sources. In communicating their own stories, producers actively intervene in the meanings of earlier recordings and offer audiences the opportunity to recombine these fragments in their own ways. While chronological histories often focus on linear progressions of technique, technology, and content, a sedimentary history of hip-hop would foreground the processes through which producers, DJs, and MCs actively entangle past and present, making new music and new stories in conversation with the recorded past.

A Gravitational History: The Blues

Writing about the blues in the context of African American expressive practices as a whole, Samuel Floyd writes, "There were blues songs about voodoo, estrangement, sex, protest, bad luck, deceit, war, joblessness, sickness, love, health, evil, revenge, railroading, and a variety of other life experiences, some sad, others not."[32] Holding together this wide range of lyrical content is a particular performance practice and a set of standard musical forms. As a container for musical creativity, the blues is surprisingly flexible and porous, allowing for a maximum of individual expression within the constraints of the genre. Floyd writes, "Blues singers composed their songs by combining fragments and verses from the hundreds or thousands of formulas that were floating around in black communities everywhere, spread by the traveling songsters. Black creativity combined these fragments with African-American performance practices, transforming them into original works of musical poetry."[33] Each new blues performance becomes a gravitational center of its own, as musicians pull together lyrical and musical ideas into a unique expressive moment. In the earliest days of blues performance, these constellations of musical expression coalesced through in-person engagement between musicians and audiences. As the community expanded, commercial recordings enabled the eventual proliferation of blues-based styles across the world.

Blues performers include vocalists, solo guitarists and banjoists, full bands, horn players, and plenty of other musicians. From the rural, acoustic country blues of Robert Johnson and the sophisticated, jazz-tinged classic blues sung by Bessie Smith to the distorted, electric blues played by Muddy Waters and the pop-tinged blues-rock of Susan Tedeschi, many subgenres of the blues have emerged as gravitational centers of their own. But each of these communities of musicians forms around a central ideal of the blues as a distinctive performance practice and a repetitious form, most often built on a twelve-measure harmonic cycle. The strong pull of those foundational principles and structures holds together an entire galaxy of styles and performers. While chronological histories might exclude artists and practices that push beyond some perceived stylistic barrier, a gravitational history of the blues would reveal how musicians from wildly different backgrounds, and pursuing very distinct goals, could all orbit the same star.

A Concentric History: Jazz

Like many musical communities, jazz scenes are built on the interlocking influences of a variety of participants. Improvising musicians are able to assemble into groups through the hard work of bandleaders and venue owners. Their work is captured by recording engineers and released by established record labels. Audiences and fans purchase recordings and concert tickets, sustaining an economy that supports musicians, venues, and labels alike. Journalists, critics, and historians contextualize the work of all of these participants, promoting individual musicians and ensembles and gradually shaping the stories that we tell about jazz history and culture. Imagine all of these groups of participants as a series of concentric rings around the ever-changing idea of "jazz," pushing and pulling from different aesthetic, commercial, and social contexts. Improvising musicians interact with each other in the midst of a pressure cooker of cross-influences, and their collaborative work is stretched, squeezed, and ultimately transformed through those layers of context, responsibility, interpretation, and choice.

At different points in the history of recorded jazz, participants in the scene have interacted in very different ways, and their complex interactions have always defined the style, the ethic, and the story of the music. As one small example of a concentric history at work, consider the changing role of jazz drummers. Drummers have chosen to accompany soloists in very different ways based on the stylistic expectations of bandleaders and audiences, as well as the limitations of available technology. Their choices are informed by the venues in which they may be performing, whether in small clubs built for close listening or in giant ballrooms made for dancing. They can push soloists to "stretch out" in very different ways depending on their recording format; the seventy-eight RPM shellac records that dominated the early days of jazz recording could only hold about three minutes of music; thirty-three RPM LPs extended that to twenty-five minutes per side. CDs can hold up to seventy-four minutes of uninterrupted music, and in the age of digital releases, recording time is only limited by available hard-drive storage. At the same time, the creative impulses of jazz drummers—in collaboration with their bandmates—have pushed audiences to explore new styles while driving manufacturers to develop new recording and playback technologies. While chronological histories often focus on the linear progression of style through the innovations of individual soloists and groups, a concentric history of jazz would demonstrate how musicians negotiate the spaces between competing pressures and expectations, continually under negotiation and emerging through improvisation.[34]

A Spiral History: Pop

Over the last century, pop music has continually turned back toward itself in search of inspiration. We have heard musicians apply new technologies and new contexts to old styles, morphing blues into rock 'n' roll, disco into house, punk into grunge. Simon Reynolds argues that this "retromania" reached its peak in the first decade of the twenty-first century, writing:

> It seemed like everything that ever was got its chance to come back at some point during the 2000s. Decades usually have a retro twin:

the seventies looked like the fifties; in the eighties you had multiple different versions of the sixties vying for attention; and then seventies music started to get rediscovered in the nineties. True to form, and right on cue, the noughties kicked off with an eighties electropop renaissance and was soon followed by a separate but parallel retro craze for post-punk. But the noughties music scene had countless other retro sectors drawing heavily on the pre-eighties, from the freak folkers to neo-psychedelic bands like Dungen to the garage-punk revival (a re-revival, actually). The pop present was caught in the crossfire of revival simultaneity, with shrapnel from multiple different pasts whizzing past our ears at any given point.[35]

Participating in a "revival" doesn't necessarily mean that the music is stuck in the past. Pop musicians often use old recordings as a springboard to new work, mining the past for big ideas and tiny details that can resonate with modern audiences. Distinct from the work of the hip-hop producers discussed previously, this resonance with the past must be fully embodied by musicians in the present. While their work contains the echoes of distant sounds, those traces must be re-sounded through performance. Because of the ubiquity and persistence of recordings, the inspiration of the past is never too far away. Because of the availability and portability of recording equipment and music production software, the future is at our fingertips. While chronological histories often foreground various "firsts," a spiral history of pop would show how the music moves forward by reaching back.

This is a story about how we tell stories. These stories teach us about ourselves and regulate the ways that we interact with and participate in this mediated world of music. The assumptions on which we built our stories once upon a time are not quite as meaningful today as they once were, largely because our interactions with music have changed so dramatically. Through recordings, music circulates quickly and broadly, reaching listeners in all corners of the world instantaneously but not equitably. As a result, our musical communities have organized themselves in ways that are fluid, contingent, and decentralized.

Different musical communities require different structures and different assumptions in order to tell their stories. The straight line that has quietly organized our understanding of history for the last two centuries was never straight, nor was it a line at all. This history is better imagined as a dense and expansive web, where disparate sounds are never too distant and every listener is free to follow their own path. This is a history that is alive, just waiting to be discovered.

NOTES

1. Pearl Jam, "Spin the Black Circle (Remastered)," YouTube, November 8, 2014, https://www.youtube.com/watch?v=T3oMcrqDn_4.
2. Much music of the last century is built on repetition or the assumption of repeated listening, from the dense serialism of mid-century composers to the loop-based works of minimalism and hip-hop. For further reading, see Mark Katz, "Causes," in *Capturing Sound: How Technology Has Changed Music* (Berkeley: University of California Press, 2004), 8–47.
3. Theodor Adorno, "On the Fetish-Character in Music and the Regression of Listening," in *Essays on Music*, trans. Richard Leppert (Berkeley: University of California Press, 2002).
4. For example, Adorno writes, "The listener is converted, along his line of least resistance, into the acquiescent purchaser." See Adorno, "Fetish-Character," 291.
5. Adorno, 288.
6. Walter Benjamin, "The Work of Art in the Age of Mechanical Reproduction," in *Illuminations*, ed. Hannah Arendt, trans. Harry Zohn (New York: Schocken Books, 1968).
7. William Howland Kenney, *Recorded Music in American Life: The Phonograph and Popular Memory, 1890–1945* (Oxford: Oxford University Press, 1999).

8. Kenney, *Recorded Music*, 10.

9. Greg Milner, *Perfecting Sound Forever: An Aural History of Recorded Music* (New York: Farrar, Straus & Giroux, 2009), 13.

10. H. Stith Bennett, *On Becoming a Rock Musician* (Amherst: University of Massachusetts Press, 1980), 114.

11. Richard Middleton, *Studying Popular Music* (Milton Keynes: Open University Press, 1980), 88. More broadly, Mark Katz refers to "phonograph effects" as "the manifestations of sound recording's influence" on how we listen, how we make music, and how we share it. See Katz, *Capturing Sound*, 3.

12. The Byrds,"The Byrds—My Back Pages (1967)," YouTube, June 16, 2009, https://www.youtube.com/watch?v=h8ol4XlPJC4.

13. Christopher Small, *Musicking: The Meanings of Performing and Listening* (Middletown, CT: Wesleyan University Press, 1998), 2.

14. Rare Facts, "I Have a Dream Speech by Martin Luther King Jr. HD (subtitled) (remastered)," YouTube, November 17, 2017, https://www.youtube.com/watch?v=vP4iY1TtS3s&t=49s.

15. For more on the role of performers in this collaborative process, see Daniel Barolsky, "Roundtable: Performance as a Master Narrative in Music History," *Journal of Music History Pedagogy* 3, no. 1 (2012): 78–79.

16. Jed Rasula, "The Media of Memory: The Seductive Menace of Records in Jazz History," in *Jazz Among the Discourses*, ed. Krin Gabbard (Durham, NC: Duke University Press, 1995), 135.

17. Chanel ZERO, "Fight the Power (From "Do The Right Thing" Soundtrack)" YouTube, November 1, 2018, https://www.youtube.com/watch?v=MwR_GFbVQkQ.

18. Elijah Wald, *How the Beatles Destroyed Rock 'n' Roll: An Alternative History of American Popular Music* (Oxford: Oxford University Press, 2011).

19. Wald, *How the Beatles*, 8.

20. Michel-Rolph Trouillot, *Silencing the Past: Power and the Production of History* (Boston: Beacon Press, 1995).

21. Traveler Into the Blue, "Arthur 'Big Boy' Crudup—That's All Right," YouTube, September 24, 2013, https://www.youtube.com/watch?v=qU3ZFNIaoto.

22. As is the case with so many similar discussions of "firsts," critics have failed to reach consensus on this question. See Bob Gulla, *Icons of R&B and Soul: An Encyclopedia of the Artists Who Revolutionized Rhythm*, vol. 1 (Westport, CT: Greenwood Press, 2008), 189; Elvis Presley, "Elvis Presley—That's All Right (Audio)," YouTube, July 22, 2015, https://www.youtube.com/watch?v=DCP_g7X3InI.

23. Trouillot, *Silencing*, 26.

24. Though these narratives are deeply entwined with popular conceptions of creative genius, scholars have long challenged us to consider the myth-making process itself—even as it applies to towering figures like Beethoven and Stravinsky. Tia DeNora explores the social construction of Beethoven's reputation, revealing ways in which the composer and his patrons actively set the stage for the image of Beethoven as a transcendent figure. Similarly, Richard Taruskin has demonstrated ways in which Stravinsky carefully positioned his work in relation to both Russian traditions and cosmopolitan ideologies in order to shape his own story. DeNora, *Beethoven and the Construction of Genius: Musical Politics in Vienna, 1792–1803* (Berkeley: University of California Press, 1995). Taruskin, *Stravinsky and the Russian Traditions: A Biography of the Works Through Mavra* (Berkeley: University of California Press, 1996).

25. Johann Kroier, "Music, Global History, and Postcoloniality," *International Review of the Aesthetics and Sociology of Music* 43, no. 1 (2012): 170.

26. Journey, "Journey—Separate Ways (Worlds Apart) (Official Video—1983)," YouTube, February 26, 2010, https://www.youtube.com/watch?v=LatorN4P9aA.

27. Rich Mullinax, "HIGH FIDELITY Rob Re-Organizes His LPs," YouTube, May 1, 2012, https://www.youtube.com/watch?v=2msCS8dvSok.

28. *High Fidelity*, directed by Stephen Frears (Los Angeles: Buena Vista Pictures, 2000).

29. Kanye West, "Blood on the Leaves," YouTube, July 21, 2018, https://www.youtube.com/watch?v=KEAobtSNkpw.

30. Awkadan, "Strange Fruit," YouTube, January 20, 2014, https://www.youtube.com/watch?v=BnuEMdUUrZQ.

31. Joseph Schloss, *Making Beats: The Art of Sample-Based Hip-Hop* (Middletown, CT: Wesleyan University Press, 2004), 36–37.

32. Samuel Floyd, *The Power of Black Music: Interpreting Its History from Africa to the United States* (Oxford: Oxford University Press, 1995), 76.

33. Floyd, *The Power*.

34. For a closer look at this idea, see Nathan C. Bakkum, "A Concentric Model for Jazz History," *Journal of Music History Pedagogy* 5, no. 2 (2015): 5–22.

35. Simon Reynolds, *Retromania* (New York: Farrar, Straus & Giroux, 2011), 408–9.

FURTHER READING

Attali, Jacques. *Noise: The Political Economy of Music*. Minneapolis: University of Minnesota Press, 1985.

Barolsky, Daniel. "The Performer as Analyst." *Music Theory Online* 13, no. 1 (2007). https://mtosmt.org/issues/mto.07.13.1/mto.07.13.1.barolsky.html

Chanan, Michael. *Repeated Takes: A Short History of Recording and Its Effects on Music*. London: Verso, 1995.

Clarke, Eric F. "The Impact of Recording on Listening." *Twentieth-Century Music* 4, no. 1 (March 2007): 47–70.

Corbett, John. "Free, Single, and Disengaged: Listening Pleasure and the Popular Music Object." *October* 54 (Autumn 1990): 79–101.

Day, Timothy. *A Century of Recorded Music: Listening to Musical History*. New Haven, CT: Yale University Press, 2000.

Eisenberg, Evan. *The Recording Angel: Explorations in Phonography*. New York: McGraw-Hill, 1987.

Goehr, Lydia. *The Imaginary Museum of Musical Works: An Essay in the Philosophy of Music*. Oxford: Oxford University Press, 1992.

Gracyk, Theodore A. "Adorno, Jazz, and the Aesthetics of Popular Music." *Musical Quarterly* 76/4 (Winter 1992): 526–42.

Horning, Susan Schmidt. "Engineering the Performance: Recording Engineers, Tacit Knowledge, and the Art of Controlling Sound." *Social Studies of Science* 34, no. 5 (October 2004): 703–31.

Kahn, Douglas. *Noise, Water, Meat: A History of Sound in the Arts*. Cambridge, MA: MIT Press, 1997).

Kenney, William Howland. *Recorded Music in American Life: The Phonograph and Popular Memory, 1890-1945*. New York: Oxford University Press, 1999.

Kot, Greg. *Ripped: How the Wired Generation Revolutionized Music*. New York: Scribner, 2009.

Kronengold, Charles. "Accidents, Hooks and Theory." *Popular Music* 24, no. 3 (October 2005): 381–97.

Link, Stan. "The Work of Reproduction in the Mechanical Aging of an Art: Listening to Noise." *Computer Music Journal* 25, no. 1 (Spring 2001): 34–47.

Manning, Peter. "The Influence of Recording Technologies on the Early Development of Electroacoustic Music." *Leonardo Music Journal* 13 (2003): 5–10.

Manuel, Peter. *Cassette Culture: Popular Music and Technology in North India*. Chicago: University of Chicago Press: 1993.

Milner, Greg. *Perfecting Sound Forever: An Aural History of Recorded Music*. New York: Faber & Faber, 2009.

Negus, Keith. *Music Genres and Corporate Cultures*. London: Routledge, 1999.

Paddison, Max. "The Critique Criticised: Adorno and Popular Music." *Popular Music* 2 (1982): 201–18.

Rings, Steven. "A Foreign Sound to Your Ear: Bob Dylan Performs 'It's Alright, Ma

(I'm Only Bleeding),' 1964–2009." *Music Theory Online* 19, no. 4 (December 2013): 1–39.

Sanden, Paul. *Liveness in Modern Music: Musicians, Technology, and the Perception of Performance.* New York: Routledge, 2013.

Schloss, Joseph. *Making Beats: The Art of Sample-Based Hip-Hop.* Middletown, CT: Wesleyan University Press, 2004.

Smith, Ayana. "Blues, Criticism, and the Signifying Trickster." *Popular Music* 24, no. 2 (May 2005): 179–91.

Sterne, Jonathan. *MP3: The Meaning of a Format.* Durham, NC: Duke University Press, 2012.

Wang, Oliver, Wang. *Legions of Boom: Filipino American Mobile DJ Crews in the San Francisco Bay Area.* Durham, NC: Duke University Press, 2015.

Waxer, Lise. *The City of Musical Memory: Salsa, Record Grooves, and Popular Music in Cali, Colombia.* Middletown, CT: Wesleyan University Press, 2002.

Zak, Albin. *The Poetics of Rock: Cutting Tracks, Making Records.* Berkeley: University of California Press, 2001.

Printed in the USA
CPSIA information can be obtained
at www.ICGtesting.com
CBHW072051160924
14314CB00001B/1